Knit & Crochet

Ponchos, Wraps, Capes & Shrugs!

EDITED BY

Edie Eckman

Storey Publishing

The mission of Storey Publishing is to serve our customers by publishing practical information that encourages personal independence in harmony with the environment.

Edited by Nancy D. Wood and Gwen Steege
Art direction and cover design by Kent Lew
Text design and production by Jennifer Jepson Smith
Cover and interior photographs by Kevin Kennefick;
except on pages 6, 7, 16, 17, 20, 21, 24, 25, 28, 29, 35, 36, 37, 38, 42, 48, 55, 58, 60, 65, 68, 69, 73, 77, 88, 97, 105 by Adam Mastoon, and on page 8 by Zeva Oelbaum
Project styling by Wendy Scofield
Illustrations by Brigita Fuhrmann
Technical editing by Dee Neer
Indexed by Susan Olason

Printed in Hong Kong by Elegance
10 9 8 7 6 5 4 3 2 1

Library of Congress Cataloging-in-Publication Data

Knit & crochet ponchos, wraps, capes & shrugs! / edited by Edie Eckman.
    p. cm.
Includes index.
ISBN-13: 978-1-58017-621-7 (diecut hardcover : alk. paper)
ISBN-10: 1-58017-621-6 (diecut hardcover : alk. paper)

TT825.K62247 2005
746.43'0432—dc22

                                    2005023113

Contents

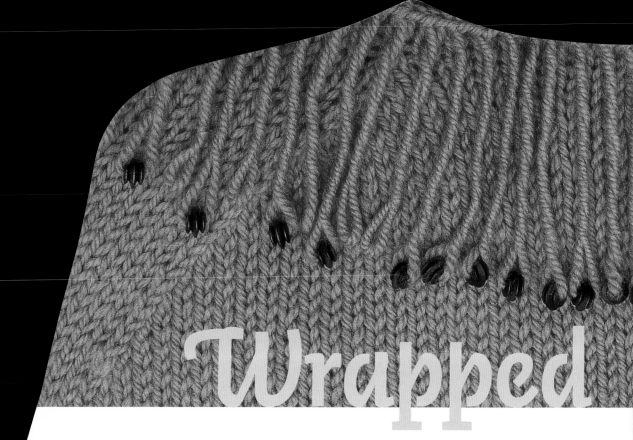

Wrapped

It's no secret that wraps are hot fashion news. Novice and experienced knitters alike are making scarves, ponchos, and shawls as fast as they can. And let's not forget the crocheters! A whole new generation is discovering fresh ways to ply its hooks.

In this book we offer a selection of wraps with something for everyone. Novice knitters will discover that the Mossy Stole or Electric Cowgirl is well within their abilities, and crocheters will find Meg's Poncho easy to stitch. More advanced knitters will be delighted with the knitterly details found in the Snug Fall Cozy and the engineering marvel that is the Aran Poncho. We haven't forgotten youthful tastes, either: What young knitter can resist the Rainbow Poncho, with its

matching gauntlets and leggings? What young crocheter will pass up the hip, lightweight Coral Capelet?

If you've never picked up a crochet hook or knitting needles, you'll have to do a bit of homework before tackling these projects. There simply isn't room enough for introductory knitting instructions, crochet instructions, and projects, too, all in one book! However, if you know the basics, you'll do fine. Along the way you may learn some new tricks. If you come

in Style

across a technique that is unfamiliar to you, we've aimed to provide enough detail for you to follow the instructions with confidence. We've included illustrations and added charts where appropriate. You can also refer to the illustrated glossary in the back to refresh your memory of basic terms.

Although there are standard guidelines that define skill levels, we find them to be somewhat arbitrary and have not rated the projects. What one person finds difficult, another may find easy. You may deem it a breeze to work several cable patterns at once (considered an advanced skill) yet get all tangled up in double-pointed needles (an intermediate skill). Besides, never underestimate the value of spunk and determination. If you fall in love with a project and are determined to see it through, you can do it! If you get stuck on an instruction you don't understand, you may need a hint from an experienced friend — or try doing a search on the Internet for information on particular stitches or techniques. But please don't hold yourself back from attempting something that may seem beyond your ability. You might just surprise yourself.

Now, read a few notes and choose your favorite project. Pick up your yarn and your tool of choice — hook or needles — and soon you'll be wrapped in style!

Yarn Basics

Yarns fit into broad weight categories. The ones in this book range from light worsted weight through bulky weight, and are widely available at yarn shops around the United States. However, sometimes yarns are discontinued, or you might prefer to use yarn with a different texture or color. The chart (right) offers information that will help you select appropriate substitutes. First review the information on the yarn indicated in the pattern, then find another yarn with a similar weight. When making substitutions, it is especially important to check your gauge before you begin the project.

WASTE YARN

Waste yarn is yarn meant to be removed and discarded at a later point in the pattern. It should be similar in weight to the main yarn used in the project and it should be smooth; fuzzy yarns may leave undesired little bits of fluff. If you are going to be picking up stitches held by waste yarn, you may want to use a highly contrasting color to make the stitches easier to see.

Waste yarn is used several times in this book: for the crocheted cast-on in the Snug Fall Cozy and Rainbow Poncho, and as a stitch holder for a large number of stitches in the Aran Poncho.

Standard Yarn Weights

The following information was compiled by the Craft Yarn Council. For more information on standards and guidelines for crochet and knitting, visit the Web site at www.yarnstandards.com.

Yarn Weight Symbol & Category Names	3 LIGHT	4 MEDIUM	5 BULKY	6 SUPER BULKY
Type of Yarns in Category	DK, Light Worsted	Worsted, Afghan, Aran	Chunky, Craft, Rug	Bulky, Roving
Knit Gauge Range* in Stockinette Stitch to 4 inches	21–24 sts	16–20 sts	12–15 sts	6–11 sts
Recommended Needle in Metric Size Range	3.75–4.5 mm	4.5–5.5 mm	5.5–8 mm	8 mm and larger
Recommended Needle in US Size Range	5–7	7–9	9–11	11 and larger
Crochet Gauge* Ranges in Single Crochet to 4 inches	12–17 sts	11–14 sts	8–11 sts	5–9 sts
Recommended Hook in Metric Size Range	4.5–5.5 mm	5.5–6.5 mm	6.5–9 mm	9 mm and larger
Recommended Hook in US Size Range	7–I/9	I/9–K/10.5	K/10.5–M/13	to M/13 and larger

*Guidelines only: Information above reflects the most commonly used gauges and needle or hook sizes for specific yarn categories.

Needle Numbers

Knitting needles come in numbered sizes, with the US, UK, and metric systems all using a different range of numbers. How's that for confusion! Luckily, most needles have both US and metric equivalents on them. If you have a pattern that indicates using UK needles, just use this handy chart for the conversions.

US	Metric	Old UK
0	2 mm	14
1	2.25 mm	13
	2.5 mm	
2	2.75 mm	12
	3 mm	11
3	3.25 mm	10
4	3.5 mm	
5	3.75 mm	9
6	4 mm	8
7	4.5 mm	7
8	5 mm	6
9	5.5 mm	5
10	6 mm	4
10½	6.5 mm	3
	7 mm	2
	7.5 mm	1
11	8 mm	0
13	9 mm	00
15	10 mm	000

Hook Conversion

In the US, hooks are sized in either letters, B through S, or numbers, 1 through 16. In the metric and English equivalents, only numbers are used. The patterns in this book give both US sizes and the metric equivalent.

Approximate Hook Sizes

US	Metric	UK
B/1	2.5 mm	12
C/2	3 mm	11
D/3	3.25 mm	10
E/4	3.5 mm	9
F/5	4 mm	8
G/6	4.25 mm	7
7	4.5 mm	7
H/8	5 mm	6
I/9	5.5 mm	5
J/10	6 mm	4
K/10.5	7 mm	3
L/11	8 mm	–
M/13	9 mm	–
N/15	10 mm	–
P/16	15 mm	–
Q	16 mm	–
S	19 mm	–

The Importance of Gauge

In most things knitted or crocheted, gauge is critical. You must match your number of stitches per inch to the gauge given in the pattern in order to have the finished item be the correct size.

To determine your gauge, make a swatch using the same stitch, yarn, and needles or hook you plan to use in the project. Make your swatch at least 5" or 6" square. When you have completed the swatch, block it first (see instructions on page 12), then place it flat on a table. Using a ruler, count the number of stitches within a 4" span. Do not count from the edges; instead, count the stitches in the middle of the swatch.

■ If you have the same number of stitches per 4" as your pattern states, terrific! You can start stitching your project.

■ If you have fewer stitches than the number called for, rework your swatch on smaller needles or hook and repeat the process until you match the gauge.

■ If you have more stitches than you want, rework the swatch on larger needles or hook and repeat until you have the right number of stitches.

Sometimes you can match the stitch gauge but have difficulty with the row gauge. In most of these patterns, row gauge is not as critical as stitch gauge. There are a few patterns in which matching the stated gauge is not vital, but a different gauge might make a difference in the amount of yarn you need. If you have a different gauge on these items, don't be surprised if you need more or less yarn than the instructions call for.

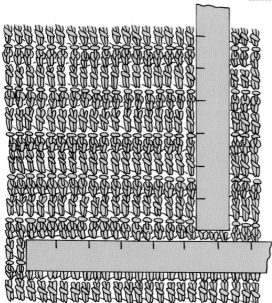

This crocheted swatch is being measured for the number of stitches (across) and the number of rows (up and down). Gauge is commonly counted per four inches, but this can vary. Check each pattern for specifics.

Stitch Charts

Used primarily for knitting, stitch charts provide visual cues that enhance or replace text instructions. Some people prefer charts alone; some prefer text instructions. Many use both, following one format until they encounter difficulties, then switching to the other to clarify the directions. Stitch charts are also used for crochet when showing a particular color pattern. This book uses primarily text instructions, but sometimes a chart is added when a pattern needs clarification.

Charts represent the right side of the fabric. Each square represents a stitch; each stitch symbol is explained in a key. Follow the chart by reading left to right or right to left as you work your way back and forth across the rows. When working in the round, read all rounds from right to left. The number for each row being worked is on the side where that row begins.

Project Symbols

On the first page of each project is one of the following icons:

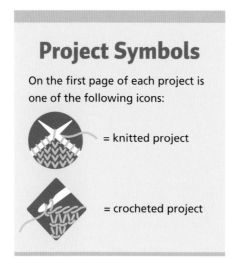

= knitted project

= crocheted project

Blocking

Blocking is a method of setting stitches and finishing the fabric. Proper blocking can make the difference between an elegant handcrafted garment and something that looks "homemade." Not all crocheted items need blocking, as they tend to hold their shape better than knitted projects. However, for the best results, we recommend blocking any projects you make from this book. *Note:* Do not block ribbing, and be especially careful with highly textured patterns, as you do not want to ruin them by blocking too severely. For example, take care when blocking cabled patterns like the Aran Poncho and the Upcountry Poncho.

The correct blocking method depends on the fiber content of your yarn; consult the instructions on the yarn band. Be sure to practice blocking on your swatch before trying it on your almost finished project!

For yarns made of animal fibers (wool, mohair), you can usually steam-block, as follows:

■ Lay the piece(s) flat on flat surface such as an ironing board or blocking and steaming pad (available in craft stores).

■ Pin the pieces in place using rust-proof pins (do not stretch or distort the fabric).

■ Hold a steam iron or steamer over surface of the fabric. Do not allow the iron to touch the fabric.

■ Allow the steam to saturate the fabric and then leave it alone to allow it to dry.

Making Fringe

Patterns vary as to the length, number, and thickness of each fringe tassel, but here are the basics, which apply to both knitting and crochet.

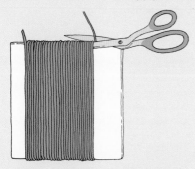

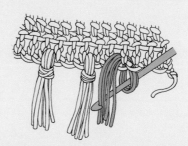

1. Check your pattern for the number and length of yarn strands needed. For instance, if you need a total of 30 strands of yarn that are 14" long, cut cardboard to 7" and wrap the yarn around it 30 times. Cut along one edge with a pair of scissors.

2. Gather the strands needed for one tassel and fold them in half. Use your crochet hook to draw the folded loop through one row of stitches. With your hook still in the loop, draw the ends through and pull firmly.

Using Markers

Stitch markers do exactly what their name implies — mark certain stitches. This can help you keep track of things, like the beginning of a round. Usually made of plastic, markers come in different colors, shapes, and sizes. Closed circles are used for knitting (slipped onto needle); open markers are usually for crochet (hung on a stitch).

knitting marker

crochet markers

Mossy Stole

Designed by Lorna Miser

Your friends won't know that this wrap is super-easy to knit; they'll just know it looks great. You'll know how splendid it feels against your skin. The color and texture evoke thoughts of a walk in the mossy woods. If you prefer, you can make the larger size for a plush throw.

The counterpoint of luxurious, shiny, multicolored ribbon and fluffy solid-color yarn does the work on this shawl. You could use any combination of textured and smooth worsted-weight yarn.

Finished measurements

Stole: 21" (53 cm) wide × 72" (1.8 m) long, excluding fringe
Throw: 42" (107 cm) wide × 60" (1.5 m) long, excluding fringe

Yarn

Heavy worsted-weight rayon chenille yarn, 77 yds (70 m) per 1.75 oz (50 g) ball in olive green (mc); worsted-weight, cotton-blend ribbon 110 yds (100 m) per 1.75 oz (50 g) ball in olive mix (cc)

We used Berroco, Chinchilla, 100% rayon, 1.75 oz (50 g)/77 yds (70 m)
mc = Oregano #5531, 6 balls for stole; 11 balls for throw
and Berroco Zen Colors, 55% cotton/ 45% nylon, 1.75 oz (50 g)/110 yds (100 m)
cc = Osaka Mix #8139, 3 balls for stole; 6 balls for throw

Needles

One US size 9 (5.5 mm) circular, 29" (74 cm), *or size you need to obtain gauge*

Gauge

12 stitches = 4" in Stitch Pattern
Take time to make sure your gauge is correct.

Other supplies

Large-eye yarn needle, crochet hook US size 9 (5.5 mm) for fringe

---

◆ **cc** = contrast color ◆ **K** = knit
◆ **mc** = main color ◆ **P** = purl
◆ **P2tog** = purl 2 stitches together
◆ **yo** = yarn over

Stitch Pattern

Row 1 (right side) With mc, knit.
Rows 2–6 With mc, knit.
Row 7 With cc, knit.
Row 8 (Eyelet Row) With cc, P1, yo, P2tog.
Repeat Rows 1–8 for Stitch Pattern.

KNITTING THE STOLE OR THROW	STOLE	THROW
NOTE: Carry any yarn not in use loosely up the edge of the knitting, twisting yarns to prevent long loops.		
NOTE: Count the stitches before working Row 7. It is the easiest row on which to see the stitches clearly, and to check that there is the correct number before working the Eyelet Row.		
To BEGIN: With mc, loosely cast on _____ stitches.	65	127
Start Stitch Pattern and work even until piece measures _____ from the beginning, ending with Row 6 of Stitch Pattern. Bind off all stitches loosely.	72" (1.83 m)	60" (1.52 m)
With a large-eye needle, weave in ends.		
MAKING THE FRINGE		
With cc, cut _____ strands, each 12" (30 cm) long.	195	381
Holding 3 strands together, fold fringe in half. With crochet hook, * insert hook from wrong side to right side into first st, pull through folded loop, insert ends into loop, and pull tight against edge; repeat from *, working into every other stitch along cast-on and bind-off edges. Trim fringe to desired length. (See Making Fringe on page 13.)		

STOLE SCHEMATIC

72"

21"

Lightweight yarn and a series of Eyelet Rows make this shawl a comfy favorite for summer evenings.

Faux Fur Muffler

Designed by Gwen Blakley-Kinsler, Fiber Impressions

This chic scarf would look great with jeans or dressed up with a sparkly brooch for a glamorous night on the town. The chunky, textured look is achieved by weaving a tapestry of novelty yarn through a simple mesh crochet background. Double crochet and chain stitch are the only crochet techniques you need to master.

Shown here in two hot pink yarns, this pattern will work equally well with contrasting colors or a different-textured yarn. Experiment with the yarns you have at home.

Finished measurements

Approximately 5" (12.7 cm) wide × 80" (2 m) long, including fringe

Yarn

Bulky-weight nylon yarn, 104 yds (96 m) per 1.75 oz (50 g) ball; worsted-weight cotton or cotton blend 85 yds (78 m) per 1.75 oz (50 g) skein

We used Berroco, Softy, 52% DuPont Tactel(r) Nylon, 48% nylon, 1.75 oz (50 g)/104 yds (96 m)
mc = Love Potion #2939, 5 balls
and Berroco, Cotton Twist, 70% mercerized cotton/30% rayon, worsted weight, 1.75 oz (50 g)/85 yds (78 m)
cc = Heath Pink #8366, 2 skeins

Crochet hooks

One US size H/8 (5 mm) and one US size K/10.5 (7 mm), *or size you need to obtain gauge*

Gauge

Seven ch-2 spaces = 5" Background Mesh, using cc; 60" of chain, worked with 3 strands mc = 6" of woven length. NOTE: Gauge is not crucial in this project.

Other supplies

Large-eye yarn needle, sewing needle, and matching thread

◆ **cc** = contrast color ◆ **ch** = chain
◆ **dc** = double crochet ◆ **mc** = main color

CROCHETING THE MUFFLER (BACKGROUND MESH)	
To Begin	With size H hook and cc, ch 26.
Row 1	Starting in eighth ch from hook, dc in eighth ch, * ch 2, skip 2 ch, dc in next ch; repeat from * across, turn (7 ch-2 spaces).
Row 2	Ch 5 (counts as dc, ch 2), dc in next dc, * ch 2, dc in next dc, repeat from * across, end ch 2, dc in third ch of turning ch, turn.
	Repeat Row 2 until mesh measures 62" (158 cm) from the beginning. Fasten off.
CROCHETING THE WEAVING CHAINS	
Before Beginning	Lay 3 strands of mc side by side, so that the "puffs" alternate; this will result in a fuller chain.
To Begin	With size K hook and 3 strands of mc held together, work a chain 60" (1.5 m) long. Fasten off.

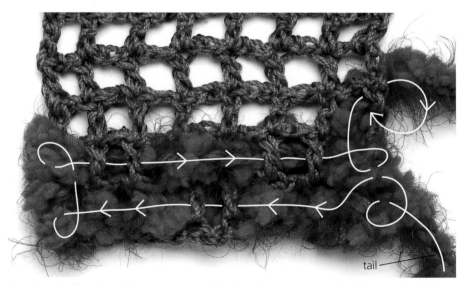

Start by winding the chain once around the first chain at one end of the mesh. Weave over two chains, under two chains, and over two chains, then wind once around the end chain. Move up one row, wind around the end chain; for this row, start by going under two chains, over two chains, and under the last two. Wind around the last chain as before. Repeat these steps all the way up the mesh.

WEAVING THE MESH	
	Starting at the lower left side of mesh, begin weaving crocheted chain through the ch-2 spaces, going over 2 dc and under 2 dc at a time (see illustration at left). When chain is completely woven in, make another 60" (1.5 m) chain with 3 strands of mc (as above). Overlap ends of chains and join with needle and matching thread. Continue to crochet and weave in chains, joining as necessary, until entire mesh is woven.
FINISHING	
	With a large-eye yarn needle, weave in ends.
Crochet fringe	Holding 3 strands of mc together, crochet six 16" (40 cm) chains. Fold chains in half and attach 3 chains, as fringe, on each end of scarf: one at each side and one in the center.
Remaining fringe	With cc, cut 48 strands, each 16" (40 cm) long. Holding 3 strands together, fold fringe in half. Using crochet hook, * insert hook from wrong side to right side into a stitch beside one of the crochet fringes, pull through the loop of folded strands, insert ends into the loop, and pull tight against edge (see Making Fringe, page 13); repeat from * attaching 6 fringes at each end of muffler between the crocheted fringe and one at each end beside the crocheted fringe (see photo below).

Make a lush fringe by alternating yarns as follows. The outer tassel is the contrasting color, the next is a chain strand made from the main color; next are three cc tassels; another mc chain; three cc tassels; one more mc chain; finish with a cc tassel.

Coral Capelet

Designed by Edie Eckman

Here's a summer wrap just perfect for layering over a T-shirt or sundress. The bright coral coordinates with many of today's tropical favorites, such as turquoise, yellow, and kiwi. The capelet is secured with a hidden hook-and-eye closure. Crochet the matching flower shown here, or substitute a real flower for a touch of panache.

Plymouth's lightweight Wildflower DK yarn is machine washable and a delight to stitch. When substituting, use a plain-textured, sport-weight yarn to show off the stitch pattern.

Finished measurements
Approximately 12" (30.5 cm) long × 52" (132 cm) around lower edge

Yarn
Double knitting-weight cotton or cotton-blend yarn, approximately 137 yds (125 m) per 1.75 oz (50 g) ball in coral and yellow

We used Plymouth Yarn, Wildflower DK, 51% cotton/49% acrylic, 1.75 oz (50 g)/137 yds (125 m)
mc = #158 (coral), 5 balls
cc = #48 (yellow), a few yards

Crochet hook
One US size F/5 (3.75 mm), *or size you need to obtain gauge*

Gauge
3 repeats = 5½"
Take time to make sure your gauge is correct.

Other supplies
Large-eye yarn needle, two pairs of hooks and eyes, sewing needle, and thread

♦ **ch** = chain ♦ **dc** = double crochet
♦ **sc** = single crochet ♦ **tr** = triple crochet

Picot Stitch

Throughout this pattern you will find instructions for making picots. In each case, use this Picot Stitch sequence.

Ch 3, slip stitch in third ch from hook.

CROCHETING THE CAPELET	
NOTE	Capelet is worked from neck to lower edge.
TO BEGIN	With mc, ch 85.
Row 1	Starting in eighth ch from hook, sc in eighth ch, ch 5, skip 3 ch, sc in next ch, * ch 6, skip 3 ch, sc in next ch, ch 5, skip 3 ch, sc in next ch; repeat from * across to last 3 ch, ch 2, skip 2 ch, dc in last ch, ch 1, turn.
Row 2	Sc in dc, in ch-5 space work 11 dc, * sc in ch-6 space, in ch-5 space work 11 dc; repeat from * across to the beginning 7 skipped chains, sc in fifth ch of 7 skipped chains, ch 4, turn.
Row 3	Skip 2 dc, * [dc in next dc, ch 1] 6 times, dc in next dc, skip (2 dc, sc, 2 dc); repeat from * across to last 3 stitches, end skip 2 dc, tr in last sc, ch 1, turn.
Row 4	Sc in tr, * ch 1, [sc in next ch-1 space, make picot using Picot Stitch] 5 times, sc in next ch-1 space, ch 1, sc between next 2 dc; repeat from * across to turning chain, ending sc in fourth ch of turning ch-4, ch 4, turn.

Row 5 (increase row)	Sc in first picot, ch 5, skip 1 picot, sc in next picot, ch 6, skip 1 picot, sc in next picot, * ch 5, sc in next picot, ch 6, skip 1 picot, sc in next picot, ch 5, skip 1 picot †, sc in next picot, ch 6, sc in next picot, ch 5, skip 1 picot, sc in next picot, ch 6, skip 1 picot, sc in next picot; repeat from * 4 more times, ending last repeat at †, sc in last picot, ch 2, tr in last stitch, turn.
Row 6	Sc in tr, in ch-5 space work 11 dc; * sc in ch-6 space, in ch-5 space work 11 dc; repeat from * across, end sc in top of turning ch, ch 4, turn.
Rows 7 and 8	Repeat Rows 3 and 4.
Row 9 (increase row)	Sc in first picot, ch 5, skip 1 picot, sc in next picot, ch 6, skip 1 picot, sc in next picot, [ch 5, sc in next picot, ch 6, skip 1 picot, sc in next picot, ch 5, skip 1 picot †, sc in next picot, ch 6, sc in next picot, ch 5, skip 1 picot, sc in next picot, ch 6, skip 1 picot, sc in next picot] 3 times; ch 5, sc in next picot, (ch 6, skip 1 picot, sc in next picot) 2 times; repeat [to] 4 times, ending last repeat at †, end sc in last picot, ch 2, tr in last stitch, ch 1, turn.
Row 10	Sc in dc, in ch-5 space work [dc, (ch 1, dc) 5 times], * sc in ch-6 space, in ch-5 space work [dc (ch 1, dc) 5 times] †; repeat from * 9 times, sc in ch-6 loop, ch 5, repeat * to † 11 times, end sc in top of turning ch, ch 4, turn.

Each row of crochet is connected to the second and fourth picot of the preceding row.

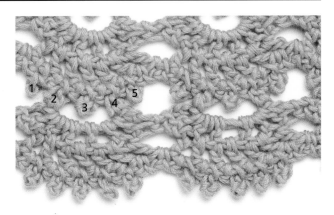

Row 11	Skip 1 dc, * [dc in next dc, ch 1, dc in ch-1 space, ch 1] 3 times, dc in next dc †, skip (dc, sc, dc) **; repeat from * 9 times; repeat * to † once, [(dc, ch 1) 4 times, dc] in ch-5 space, skip (sc and 1 dc); repeat * to ** 10 times; repeat * to † once, end tr in last sc, ch 1, turn.
Row 12	Sc in tr, * ch 1, [sc in next ch-1 space, make picot using Picot Stitch] 5 times, sc in ch-1 space †, ch 1, sc between next 2 dc **; repeat from * 10 times, ch 1, [sc in next ch-1 space, make picot using Picot Stitch] 3 times, sc in next ch-1 space, ch 1, sc between next 2 dc; repeat * to ** 11 times, ending last repeat at †, end sc in fourth ch of turning ch-4, ch 6, turn.
Row 13	Skip first picot, * sc in next picot, ch 5, skip 1 picot, sc in next picot, ch 6 †, skip 2 picots **; repeat from * 10 times, end last repeat at †, skip 1 picot; repeat from * to † once, skip 1 picot; repeat from * to ** 10 times, end sc in next picot, ch 5, skip 1 picot, sc in next picot, ch 2, tr in last sc, ch 1, turn.
Row 14	Sc in tr, in ch-5 space work [dc, (ch 1, dc) 5 times], * sc in ch-6 space, in ch-5 space work [dc, (ch 1, dc) 5 times]; repeat from * across, end sc in fourth ch of ch-6 turning ch, ch 4, turn.
Row 15	Skip 1 dc, * [dc in next dc, ch 1, dc in ch-1 space, ch 1] 3 times, dc in next dc †, skip (dc, sc, dc); repeat from * across, ending last repeat at †, end tr in last sc, ch 1, turn.
Row 16	Sc in tr, * ch 1, [sc in ch-1 space, make picot using Picot Stitch] 5 times, sc in ch-1 space †, ch 1, sc between next 2 dc; repeat from * across, ending last repeat at †, end sc in fourth ch of turning ch-4, ch 6, turn.
Row 17	Skip first picot, * sc in next picot, ch 5, skip 1 picot, sc in next picot †, ch 6, skip 2 picots; repeat from * across, ending last repeat at †, end ch 2, tr in last sc, ch 1, turn.
Rows 18–25	Repeat Rows 14–17 twice.
Rows 26–27	Repeat Rows 14–15.

Row 28	Repeat Row 16, omitting the (ch 6, turn) at the end of the row.
Edging	Work 2 sc in same stitch, sc evenly up right front edge, work 3 sc in corner stitch, 5 sc in each ch-loop of beginning ch, 2 sc in corner stitch, sc evenly down left front edge. Fasten off.

This version of the capelet was crocheted with 4 skeins of Classic Elite, Provence, 100% Egyptian cotton, 3.5 oz (100 g)/205 yds (187.5 m), Pure Periwinkle #51. You can also experiment with making up the flower in a contrasting color.

CROCHETING THE FLOWER	
To Begin	With cc, ch 4, join with a slip stitch to form a ring.
Round 1	Ch 1, sc in ring 10 times, join with slip stitch to ch-1. Cut cc.
Round 2	Join mc. Ch 4 (counts as sc, ch 3), * skip 1 sc, sc in next sc, ch 3; repeat from * 3 times, end join with slip stitch to first ch of ch-4.

How to Make a Flower

Round 1: Ten single crochet stitches are worked into a ring.

Round 2: A chain of stitches is worked into every other sc stitch; **Round 3** is worked into the loops formed by the chains.

Round 4 is worked behind Rounds 2 and 3, into every other sc stitch that was NOT crocheted in previous rounds.

Round 5 is worked into the loops formed by Round 4. **Round 6** (not shown) will add picots around each petal.

Round 3	* Work 5 sc in ch-3 loop, slip stitch in sc; repeat from * 4 times, end join with a slip stitch in beginning stitch.
Round 4	Ch 2, working behind stitches of Rounds 2 and 3, * sc in next unworked sc of Round 1, ch 5; repeat from * 4 times, end join with a slip stitch in beginning stitch.
Round 5	Slip stitch in ch-5 loop, ch 1, work 11 dc in ch-5 loop, * slip stitch in sc, 11 dc in next ch-5 loop; repeat from * 3 times, end join with a slip stitch in beginning stitch.
Round 6	* [Sc in next dc, make picot] 9 times, sc in next dc; repeat from * 4 times. Fasten off.
FINISHING	
	With a large-eye yarn needle, weave in ends.
	With sewing needle and matching thread, sew hooks to back of flower opposite each other on Round 1 (see photo below). Sew 1 eye to each neck edge, approximately 1" (2.5 cm) below neck edge.

Sew two hooks to the back of the flower, one on each side of Round 1 (center color). Sew the eyes to the capelet, one on each side, about one inch below the neck edge.

Rainbow Poncho

Designed by Beth Walker-O'Brien

Wrap it *all* up with this trendy set — a multicolored poncho with leggings (page 36) and gauntlets (page 38). Instructions are given in one size; continue to increase for a larger garment or stop the increase sooner for a smaller one. The poncho is worked primarily from the neck down first, then the collar is picked up at the neckline and knit in ribbing. The long color-repeats of this worsted-weight yarn create the striped design. If you'd rather, use up bits of leftover yarn in a random pattern.

Finished measurements
Approximately 16" (40.5 cm) at shoulders × 29" (73.5 cm) long

Yarn for the poncho
Worsted-weight wool or wool-blend yarn, 108 yds (100 m) per 1.75 oz (50 g) skein

We used Noro, Kureyon, 100% wool, 1.75 oz (50 g)/108 yds (100 m) #55 (green variegated), 9 skeins

Needles
US size 8 (5 mm) circular, 32" (80 cm) long
US size 10 (6 mm) circular, 32" (80 cm) long
US size 10 (6 mm) circular, 16" (40 cm) long
or sizes you need to obtain gauge

Gauge
16 stitches = 4" and 20 rows = 4" in Stockinette Stitch, using larger needles
Take time to make sure your gauge is correct.

Other supplies
Waste yarn and size J/10 (6 mm) crochet hook (for crochet cast-on), 4 stitch markers (one a different color), large-eye yarn needle, four ½" (1.25 cm) buttons, sewing needle, and matching thread

---

◆ **K** = knit ◆ **K2tog** = knit 2 stitches together (decrease) ◆ **M1-L** and **M1-R** = see Techniques on page 32. ◆ **P** = purl ◆ **P2tog** = purl 2 stitches together (decrease) ◆ **wyib** = with yarn in back ◆ **wyif** = with yarn in front ◆ **yo** = yarn over

TECHNIQUES

Crochet (Provisional) Cast-On = With waste yarn and hook, chain stitches loosely (see *chain* in glossary). Chain more than the pattern requires; extra chains are easily removed later and are good insurance. With larger 16" (40 cm) circular needle and mc, pick up the number of stitches indicated, knitting into the bumps on the back of the crocheted chain.

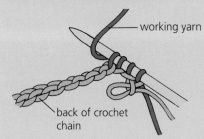

working yarn

back of crochet chain

Lifted Increase (left-slanting) = (M1-L) Insert tip of left-hand needle from front to back into the back of the stitch two rows below stitch on right-hand needle (the purl bump), lift this loop onto the left-hand needle, knit the loop, increasing 1 stitch (see *make 1* in glossary).

Lifted Increase (right-slanting) = (M1-R) Insert tip of right-hand needle from front to back into the back of the stitch below the next stitch on the left-hand needle, knit this loop, increasing 1 stitch (see *make 1* in glossary).

PONCHO SCHEMATIC

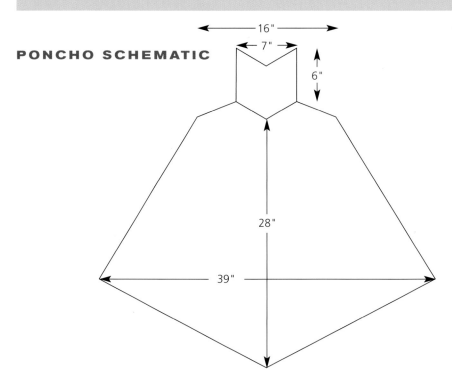

16"

7"

6"

28"

39"

KNITTING THE PONCHO BODY	
NOTE	Begin the poncho using the larger circular needle (the shorter length), then change to the longer length when the shorter one becomes uncomfortably full of stitches.
NOTE	It helps to use stitch markers (see page 13) to indicate where to increase. Use a different-color marker at the beginning of the round.
TO BEGIN	Following the instructions for Crochet (Provisional) Cast-On from page 32, cast on 80 stitches.
	Join, being careful not to twist stitches; place a marker for the beginning of the round (left shoulder).
Round 1 (setup)	* K20, place marker; repeat from * 3 times.
Round 2 (increase)	* K1, M1-L, knit to 1 stitch before next marker, M1-R, K1, slip marker; repeat from * 3 times (8 stitches increased).
Round 3	Knit.
Rounds 4–19	In Stockinette Stitch (knit every round), increase 1 stitch before and 1 stitch after each marker every other round 8 more times, ending with Round 19 (152 stitches).
Round 20	Discontinue increasing at shoulder markers as follows: * Knit to 1 stitch before marker (center front), M1-R, K1, slip marker, K1, M1-L, knit to next marker, remove marker. Knit to 1 stitch before marker (center back), M1-R, K1, slip marker, K1, M1-L, knit to next marker. Do not remove marker for beginning of round.
Round 21	Knit.
Continuing	As established, increase 1 stitch before and after front and back markers every other round until piece measures 20" (51 cm) from the beginning.

Then	Increase at front and back markers every fourth round until piece measures 28" (71 cm) from the beginning.
KNITTING THE LOWER EDGE	
	Change to smaller 32" (80 cm) circular needle and Garter Stitch.
Round 1	Purl.
Round 2	Knit.
	Repeat Rounds 1 and 2 twice, then Round 1 once.
	Bind off all stitches in pattern.
KNITTING THE COLLAR	
NOTE	The collar is worked back and forth on circular needle.
	With smaller circular needle and mc, cast on 4 stitches.
	Remove the waste yarn, placing 81 stitches from the cast-on onto the needle (NOTE: pick up the extra half-stitch) and work the stitches as follows: K1, [P2, K2] 20 times.
Continuing	Cast on 3 stitches at the end of this row (88 stitches).
Row 1 (wrong side)	Wyif, slip 1 as if to purl, work Row 1 of K2, P2 ribbing (see page 37) across to last 3 stitches, end K2, P1.
Row 2	Wyib, slip 1 as if to purl, work Row 2 of ribbing across to last 3 stitches, end P2, K1.
	Repeat Rows 1 and 2 until collar measures 1½" (3.8 cm) from beginning, end with Row 2.
Buttonhole Row	* Wyif, slip 1 as if to purl, K2, P2tog, yo, K2, continue ribbing across to last 3 stitches, end K2, P1.

	Beginning with Row 2, repeat Rows 1 and 2 for 1" (2.5 cm), end with Row 2. Repeat from * (Buttonhole Row) 3 times (4 buttonholes).
	Beginning with Row 2, repeat Rows 1 and 2 for an additional 1½" (3.8 cm).
	Bind off all stitches in pattern.
FINISHING	
	With large-eye yarn needle, weave in all ends.
	Block piece to measurements; follow instructions on yarn band.
	Overlap the cast-on stitches at the base of the neck band; with yarn needle and mc, stitch them to the body of the poncho.
	With sewing needle and matching thread, sew buttons on inside of collar, opposite buttonholes (see photograph on page 31).

Buttons are sewn to the inside of the collar. The collar can then be opened up and worn flat (see page 31) or buttoned up and turned inside out. Either way, the buttons will show on the outside.

Rainbow Leggings

Do up these leggings in the same yarn as the poncho, or choose a complementary solid color. The stretchy 2 x 2 rib allows these warmers to fit most legs.

Finished measurements
21" (53 cm) long

Yarn for the leggings
Worsted-weight wool or wool-blend yarn, approximately 108 yds (100 m) per 1.75 oz (50 g) skein

We used Noro, Kureyon, 100% wool, 1.75 oz (50 g)/108 yds (100 m) #55 (green variation), 4 skeins

Needles
One pair US size 5 (3.75 mm) straight, *or size you need to obtain gauge*
One pair US size 7 (4.5 mm) straight, *or size you need to obtain gauge*

Gauge
24 stitches = 4" and 26 rows = 4" in K2, P2 ribbing using larger needles. *Take time to make sure your gauge is correct.*

K2, P2 Ribbing

Row/Round 1: * K2, P2; repeat from * across.
Row 2: * P2, K2; repeat from * across.
Repeat Rows 1 and 2 for K2, P2 ribbing
worked straight.
Repeat Round 1 for K2, P2 ribbing worked
circular.

KNITTING THE LEGGINGS (MAKE 2)	
NOTE	Leggings are worked from ankle to upper band.
TO BEGIN	With smaller needles, cast on 42 stitches.
Row 1 (wrong side)	P1 (edge stitch), work Row 1 of K2, P2 ribbing across to last stitch, P1 (edge stitch).
Row 2	K1, work Row 2 of ribbing across to last stitch, K1.
	Repeat Rows 1 and 2 until piece measures 1" (2.5 cm) from the beginning.
Shaping the calf	Change to larger needles and continue in pattern as established, and *at the same time*, increase 1 stitch each side every 4 rows 14 times, working increased stitches in pattern as they become available (70 stitches).
Continuing	Work even until piece measures 20" (51 cm).
Knitting the band	Change to smaller needle and work in pattern for 1" (2.5 cm).
	Bind off all stitches in pattern.
FINISHING	
	With large-eye yarn needle and mc, sew back seam, matching shaping. Weave in all ends.

Matching Gauntlets

Designed by Edie Eckman

For an elegant finishing touch, make up these gauntlets with the same rainbow yarn or a complimentary color. Worked in the round, they require no shaping and little finishing.

Finished measurements
13" (33 cm) long

Yarn for the gauntlets
Worsted-weight wool or wool-blend yarn, approximately 210 yds (193 m) per 3 oz (100 g) ball

We used Plymouth, Galway, 100% wool, 3 oz (100 g)/210 yds (193 m) #127 (light green), 1 ball

Needles
One set US size 7 (4.5 mm) double pointed, *or size you need to obtain gauge*

Gauge
28 stitches = 4" and 23 rows = 4" in K2, P2 ribbing (relaxed). *Take time to make sure your gauge is correct.*

Picot Bind-Off

Bind off number of stitches indicated in instructions, * return stitch on right-hand needle to left-hand needle, [insert tip of right-hand needle between first and second stitches on left-hand needle, yarn over and knit up a stitch, place stitch on left-hand needle) 3 times, bind off 5 stitches; repeat from * 10 times (11 picots made), bind off remaining stitches.

KNITTING THE GAUNTLETS (MAKE 2)	
To Begin	With double-pointed needles, cast on 40 stitches. Join, being careful not to twist stitches; place a marker for beginning of round.
Round 1	Work Round 1 of K2, P2 ribbing (see page 37).
Continuing	As established, work even until piece measures 9½" (24 cm) from the beginning.
Divide for thumb slit	K1, turn.
Row 1	Slip 1, work as established across to last stitch, end P1.
Row 2	Slip 1, work as established across to last stitch, end K1.
Continuing	Repeat Rows 1 and 2 until thumb slit measures 1½" (3.8 cm), end Row 2. Do not turn at the end of last row.
Continuing	In rounds, work in pattern established until piece measures 13" (33 cm) from the beginning.
Working edging	Left gauntlet: Bind off 2 stitches in pattern, work Picot Bind-Off.
	Right gauntlet: Bind off 18 stitches in pattern, work Picot Bind-Off.
FINISHING	
	With large-eye yarn needle, weave in all ends.

Cinderella Cape

Designed by Kathleen Power Johnson

After Cinderella met her prince, she might have worn this feather-light concoction. Romantic ruffles envelope your shoulders, while the fluffy mohair yarn warms without weight. The lacy stitch is quick and fun to do. Choose an eye-catching pin at the neck to secure the front and adjust the fit.

If you like a more generous ruffle, try the periwinkle version on page 45. Substitute any light and lofty yarn that works to a similar gauge.

Size One size

Finished measurements
Approximately 47" (119 cm) around shoulders × 10" (25.5 cm) long

Yarn
Bulky-weight, mohair-blend yarn, approximately 975 yds (891 m) per 7 oz (198 g) skein in blue or white

We used Lorna's Laces, Heaven, 90% kid mohair, 10% nylon, 7 oz (198 g)/975 yds (891 m)
Natural #0ns, 1 skein
or
Periwinkle #49ns, 1 skein

NOTE: The cape uses only 3.5 oz (100 g) of yarn; you can make two out of one skein.

Crochet hook
One US size M/13 (9 mm), *or size you need to obtain gauge*

Gauge
3 dc = 2" and 3 rows = 2" in Puff Stitch Pattern
Take time to make sure your gauge is correct.

Other supplies
Large-eye yarn needle, shawl pin

◆ **ch** = chain ◆ **dc** = double crochet
◆ **hdc** = half double crochet
◆ **sc** = single crochet ◆ **yo** = yarn over

CAPE SCHEMATIC

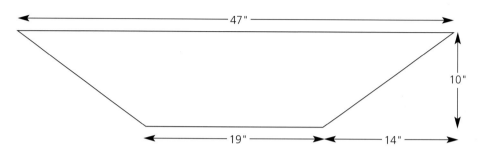

← 47" →

19" ← → 14"

10"

Pattern Stitches

PUFF STITCH
(Yo, insert hook into stitch, yo and pull loop through) 3 times, yo and pull through 7 loops, close with ch 1.

PARTIAL PUFF STITCH
Ch 2, (yo and pull up a loop in same stitch) twice, yo and through 5 loops (counts as 1 Puff Stitch).

CROCHETING THE CAPE	
NOTE	Ch 3 counts as 1 dc throughout.
TO BEGIN	Ch 36 loosely.
Row 1 (right side)	Starting in second ch from hook, sc in second ch and in each chain across, turn (35 stitches).
Row 2	Work Partial Puff Stitch, work 1 Puff Stitch in each of next 5 stitches, 2 Puff Stitches in next stitch, * work 1 Puff Stitch in

	each of next 6 stitches, 2 Puff Stitches in next stitch; repeat from * 2 more times, work 1 Puff Stitch in each of next 7 stitches, turn (39 stitches).
Rows 3, 5, 7, 9, and 11	Ch 3, dc between each Puff Stitch, dc in top of Puff Stitch, turn.
Row 4	Work Partial Puff Stitch, work 1 Puff Stitch in each of next 6 stitches, 2 Puff Stitches in next stitch, * work 1 Puff Stitch in each of next 7 stitches, 2 Puff Stitches in next stitch; repeat from * 2 more times, work 1 Puff Stitch in each of next 7 stitches, turn (43 stitches).
Row 6	Work Partial Puff Stitch, work 1 Puff stitch in each of next 7 stitches, 2 Puff Stitches in next stitch, * work 1 Puff Stitch in each of next 8 stitches, 2 Puff Stitches in next stitch; repeat from * 2 more times, work 1 Puff Stitch in each of next 8 stitches, turn (48 stitches).
Row 8	Work Partial Puff Stitch, work 1 Puff Stitch in each of next 8 stitches, 2 Puff Stitches in next stitch, * work 1 Puff Stitch in each of next 9 stitches, 2 Puff Stitches in next stitch; repeat from * 2 more times, work 1 Puff Stitch in each of next 9 stitches, turn (53 stitches).
Row 10	Work Partial Puff Stitch, work 1 Puff Stitch in each of next 9 stitches, 2 Puff Stitches in next stitch, * work 1 Puff Stitch in each of next 10 stitches, 2 Puff Stitches in next stitch; repeat from * 2 more times, work 1 Puff Stitch in each of next 10 stitches, turn (58 stitches).
Row 12	Work Partial Puff Stitch, work 1 Puff Stitch in each of next 10 stitches, 2 Puff Stitches in next stitch, * work 1 Puff Stitch in each of next 11 stitches, 2 Puff Stitches in next stitch; repeat from * 2 more times, work 1 Puff Stitch in each of next 11 stitches, turn (63 stitches).
Row 13	Ch 3, dc between each Puff Stitch, dc in top of Puff Stitch (64 stitches). Fasten off.

CROCHETING THE RUFFLES, WHITE VERSION	
To Begin	With right side facing, join yarn at corner of beginning chain.
Round 1	Working along opposite side of beginning ch, ch 3, [sc, ch 2, sc, ch 1, sc] in first stitch, ch 1 [sc, ch 1] in each stitch of beginning ch; work [sc, ch 1, sc, ch 2, (sc, ch 1) 2 times] in corner stitch (corner made); [sc, ch 1] down center front, make corner; [(sc, ch 1) 2 times] in each stitch of lower edge, make corner; (sc, ch 1) up center front, end join with a slip stitch in ch-3 space.
Round 2	Ch 3 (counts as hdc, ch 1), * [hdc, ch 2, hdc, ch 1] in corner ch-2 space (corner made); [hdc, ch 1] in each ch-1 space around, working corners in ch-2 spaces, end join with a slip stitch in ch-3 space.
Round 3	Ch 4 (counts as dc, ch 1), [dc, ch 1] in same ch-space, [dc, ch 2, dc, ch 1] in ch-2 space (corner made), * [dc, ch 1] twice in each ch-1 space to corner, make corner; repeat from * once, [dc, ch 1] in each ch-1 space to corner, make corner; [dc, ch 1] twice in each ch-1 space to beginning of round, end join with a slip stitch in ch-4 space.
Round 4	Ch 4 (counts as dc, ch 1), [dc, ch 1] in next ch-1 space, make corner; [sc, ch 1] in each ch-1 space to corner, make corner; [dc, ch 1] in each ch-1 space to corner, make corner; [dc, ch 1] in each ch-1 space to beginning of round, end join with a slip stitch to ch-4 space. Fasten off.
CROCHETING RUFFLES, PERIWINKLE VERSION	
To Begin	With right side facing, join yarn at corner of beginning chain.
Round 1	Work as for white version.
Round 2	Ch 3 (counts as hdc, ch 1), [hdc, ch 1, hdc, ch 2, (hdc, ch 1) 2 times] in ch-2 space (corner made), * [hdc, ch 1] in each ch-1 space to corner, make corner; repeat from * 2 times, [hdc, ch 1] in each ch-1 space to beginning of round, end join with a slip stitch in ch-3 space.

Round 3	Ch 4 (counts as dc, ch 1), (dc, ch 1) in same ch-1 space, [dc, ch 1] 2 times in next ch-1 space, [dc, ch 1, dc, ch 2, (dc, ch 1) 2 times] in ch-2 space (corner made), * [dc, ch 1] 2 times in each ch-1 space to corner, make corner; repeat from * once, [dc, ch 1] in each ch-1 space across lower edge, make corner; [dc, ch 1] 2 times into each ch-1 space to beginning of round, end join with a slip stitch in ch-4 space.
Rounds 4 and 5	Ch 4 (counts as dc, ch 1), [dc, ch 1] in each ch-1 space around, working corners in ch-2 spaces, end join with a slip stitch in ch-4 space. Fasten off.

Here's the same pattern, same yarn, in a different color, with a longer ruffle and a sideways drape.

Maid Marian Cloak

Designed by Kathleen Power Johnson

The rich red of this heavy cloak will turn heads as you stroll in the woods with your own Robin Hood. Vertical bands of clustered stitches highlight the shaping, while welts at the neck and cuffs keep out chilly breezes. The superwash wool makes for easy care, but any worsted-weight yarn will work nicely. Knit in one piece for minimal finishing, this challenging design is more appropriate for experienced knitters.

Size Small/medium (large/extra large)

Finished measurements

Width: 50½" (128 cm), 59¼" (150.5 cm) at lower edge

Length: 21" (53 cm), 24" (61 cm)

Yarn

Worsted-weight wool or wool blend, approximately 65 yds (59 m) per 1.75 oz (50 g) ball in dark red

We used Classic Elite Yarns, Bazic Wool, 100% superwash wool, 1.75 oz (50 g)/65 yds (59 m) Barn Red #2958, 25 (27) balls

Needle

One US size 8 (5 mm) circular, 32" (80 cm) long, *or size you need to obtain gauge*

Gauge

16 stitches = 4" and 32 rows = 4" in Garter Stitch (purl every row)

Take time to make sure your gauge is correct.

Other supplies

Large-eye yarn needle, one US size H/8 (5 mm) crochet hook, 12 (14) ⅝" buttons

---

◆ **C2F, PW2,** and **Cluster** = see Techniques on page 48. ◆ **ch** = chain ◆ **P2tog** = purl 2 together ◆ **P2tog-tbl** = purl 2 stitches together through the back loops ◆ **sc** = single crochet ◆ **ssk** = slip, slip, knit

TECHNIQUES

C2F = (2-stitch left-slanting twist) K2tog but do not slip stitches off left-hand needle, knit the first stitch, slip both stitches off left-hand needle.

Cluster Group = each group of 2 knit stitches that form the twist and cluster bands. To make a cluster, slip next 6 stitches, one at a time purlwise, to right-hand needle, dropping extra loops, return stitches to left-hand needle; working into all 6 stitches as a group, K1, P1 into the group of stitches (2 stitches remain).

PW2 = Insert right-hand needle into stitch as if to purl, wrap yarn twice around needle and complete the purl stitch.

KNITTING THE CLOAK	S/M	L/XL
NOTE: Cloak is worked from the lower edge to neck edge in 13 segments, separated by twist and cluster bands.		
To BEGIN: Cast on ____ stitches.	357	409
Row 1 (right side): P2, * K2, P ____, C2F, P ____; repeat from * across, ending last repeat P2.	25	29
Row 2: Purl.		
Row 3: P2, * C2F, P ____, (K1, P1, K1) into each of next 2 stitches, P____; repeat from * across, ending last repeat P2.	25	29
You will have ____ stitches.	383	437
Row 4: P2, * K6, P ____; repeat from * across, end P ____.	52 29	60 33
Row 5: P2, * K2, P ____, PW2 into each of next 6 stitches, P ____; repeat from * across, ending last repeat P2.	25	29

	S/M	L/XL
Row 6: P2, Cluster Group, * P _____, cluster; repeat from * across, end P _____. _____stitches remain.	52 29 357	60 33 409
Row 7: P2, * C2F, P _____, K2, P _____; repeat from * across, ending last repeat P2.	25	29
Rows 8, 10, 12: Purl.		
Row 9: Repeat Row 1.		
Row 11: Repeat Row 7.		
Row 13: P2, * (K1, P1, K1) into each of next 2 stitches, P_____, C2F, P_____; repeat from * across, ending last repeat P2.	25	29
You will have _____ stitches.	383	437
Row 14: P_____,	29	33
K6, * P_____, K6; repeat from * across, ending P2.	52	60
Row 15: P2, * PW2 into each of next 6 stitches, P _____, K2, P_____; repeat from * across, ending last repeat P2.	25	29
Row 16: P_____, cluster,	29	33
* P _____, cluster; repeat from * across, end P2.	52	60
Row 17: P2, * K2, P2tog, P _____, P2tog-tbl, C2F, P2tog, P _____, P2tog-tbl; repeat from * across, end K2, P2tog,	21	25
P_____, C2F, P2.	23	27
Row 18: Purl.		
Row 19: P2, * C2F, P_____, K2, P_____; repeat from * across, end C2F, P_____, K2, P2.	23	27

	S/M	L/XL
Row 20: Purl.		
Repeat Rows 1–20, maintaining pattern and decreasing at each side of Garter Stitch segments as on Row 17 on Rows ____, then every ____ rows ____ times, then every 4 rows 4 times. Work 1 row even. Bind off remaining stitches.	37, 57, 77 26 3	35, 53 20 6
RIGHT FRONT BAND		
NOTE: With right side facing, segments are numbered, from right to left, 1 through 13.		
With right side facing, pick up and knit ____ stitches.	84	96
WELT		
Row 1 (wrong side): Knit.		
Row 2: Purl.		
Row 3: Knit.		
Row 4: Knit.		
Row 5: Purl.		
Row 6: Knit.		
Repeat Rows 1–6 once, then Rows 1–3 once. Bind off.		
COLLAR		
With right side facing, work crochet slip stitch around neckline, including top of welt, fasten off.		
Pick up and knit 73 stitches into the slip-stitch edge, placing a marker at the sixth and twelfth Cluster Groups.		

	S/M	L/XL
Work Welt Rows 1–6 four times, at the same time working ssk before each marker and K2tog after each marker on Row 4 three times (61 stitches remain).		
Work Welt Rows 1–3 once more.		
Bind off remaining stitches.		
LEFT FRONT BAND		
With right side facing, work 2 rows of sc along front edge including collar. Mark button placement as follows: 3 buttons on collar, the first ½" (1.25 cm) from the top edge, the third at the beginning of the collar; space remaining ____ buttonholes every 2" (5 cm).	9	11
BUTTON LOOPS		
Mark button-loop placement to correspond to markers on left band.		
Work 2 rows sc along right front edge including collar, forming button loops as follows: sc to marked point, * ch 1, skip 1 stitch, sc to next marker; repeat from * for remaining button loops, work to end.		
CUFFS		
Place markers 4½" (11.5 cm) on either side of sixth and twelfth Cluster Groups.		
For each cuff, with right side facing, pick up and knit 36 stitches between markers. Work Rows 1–6 of welt ____ times, then Welt Rows 1–3 once.	4	3
Bind off all stitches.		
Fold cuffs in half and seam cuffs and underarms for 5" (12.7 cm).		

Electric Cowgirl

Designed by Beth Walker-O'Brien

Wear it around your neck or wrap it around your hips to bring color to a little black dress. Either way, this scarf's sexy drape and swingy fringe make it a joy to wear. Knitting doesn't get any easier than an all-over garter stitch, making this the perfect project for a new knitter. The generous fringe is made by knitting stitches, then unraveling them.

The novelty "railroad" style of yarn is available in many different colorways, so you are sure to find something that matches your mood and your wardrobe.

Finished measurements
Approximately 64" (162.5 cm) across ×
16" (41 cm) long at center, excluding fringe

Yarn
Light worsted-weight, 100% polyamide
yarn, approximately 82 yds (75 m) per
.9 oz (25 g) ball

We used Trendsetter, Binario, 100%
polyamide, .9 oz (25 g)/82 yds (75 m)
#115 Madras Multi, 4 balls

NOTE: You may need an extra ball of yarn
if your gauge is substantially different from
the stated gauge.

Needles
One pair US size 15 (10 mm), *or size you
need to obtain gauge*

Gauge
13 stitches = 4" and 12 rows = 4" in garter
stitch
NOTE: Gauge is not crucial in this project.

Other supplies
Stitch marker, stitch holder, large-eye yarn
needle

◆ **K** = knit ◆ **K1-f/b** = knit into front
loop, then back loop of next stitch
(increase) ◆ **K2tog** = knit 2 stitches
together (decrease)

KNITTING THE SCARF	
NOTE	The looped fringe (4 stitches at each side of the body of the scarf) is knit and then unraveled, row by row, and tied in an overhand knot.
TO BEGIN	Cast on 13 stitches.
SETUP	K9, place marker (see page 13), K4.
Row 1 (right side)	K4, slip marker, K1-f/b, knit to end.
Row 2	Work even in garter stitch (knit across).
Continuing	In garter stitch as established (knit every row), repeat Rows 1 and 2, increasing 1 stitch after the marker every other row until there are 60 stitches on the needle, end with a wrong-side row.
Next Row (right side)	K4, slip marker, K2tog, knit to end.
Continuing	In garter stitch, decrease 1 stitch after the marker every other row, until there are 13 stitches remaining.
	Place remaining stitches on a holder.
FINISHING	
Unraveling the fringe	Remove the first 4 stitches from the holder and pull out working end of the yarn. Working two rows at a time, drop 4 stitches (twice) and tie a knot near the body of the scarf with the resulting loop of yarn (see box on next page). Each loop of fringe should be the same length as its neighbors.
	Repeat the above instructions on the other side of the scarf, working with the last 4 stitches on the holder.
	Join yarn to remaining 5 stitches. Bind off loosely.
	With a large-eye yarn needle, weave in ends.

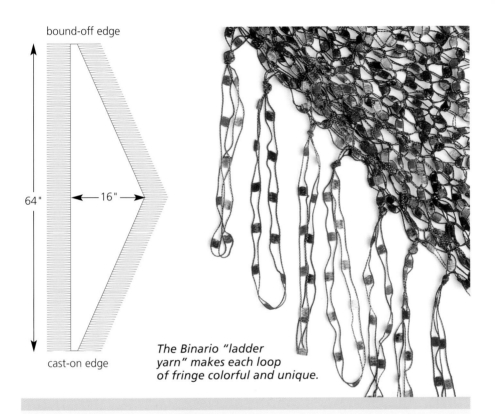

bound-off edge

64"

16"

cast-on edge

The Binario "ladder yarn" makes each loop of fringe colorful and unique.

How to Unravel Fringe

Unraveling fringe may seem complicated, but once you get the hang of it, it's easy! For this project, remove the first 4 stitches from the holder, then pull the working yarn. It will unravel as far as the holder, then stop. Pull on the live stitches in the first row; this will unravel 2 rows of stitches, then go no further. Continue on down, 2 rows at a time. Depending on the pattern, you may or may not tie a knot at the base of each loop of fringe.

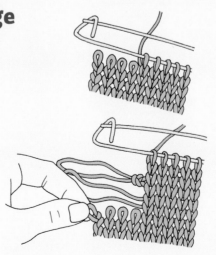

Golden Mesh Wrap

Designed by Edie Eckman

A delicate lace pattern and glitzy metallic yarn make this wrap a natural for evenings at the theater. Lacy trefoils embellish a mesh background, while bands of double crochet and a single-crochet edging add body to the fabric. Try it in a pastel cotton to wear over a sundress for a touch of style on hot summer days.

Berroco's Metallic FX yarn is a soft metallic-blend yarn with great drape. Experiment with other light worsted-weight yarns for their suitability with the stitch pattern.

Finished measurements

13" (33 cm) wide × 60 (152 cm) long or 72" (183 c) long

Yarn

Light worsted-weight rayon/metallic blend yarn, approximately 85 yds (78 m) per .9 oz (25 g) ball in gold

We used Berroco Metallic FX, 85% rayon, 15% metallic, .9 oz (25 g)/ 85 yds (78 m) Gold #1001, 6 (or 7) skeins

Crochet hook

One US size H/8 (5 mm), *or size you need to obtain gauge*

Gauge

16 stitches = 4" in double crochet
Take time to make sure your gauge is correct.

- ◆ **ch** = chain ◆ **dc** = double crochet
- ◆ **sc** = single crochet

Trefoil Stitch

To Begin: Ch 9. Starting in the eighth ch from hook, sc in eighth ch, [ch 7, sc in same stitch as previous sc] twice, sc in next ch of ch-9.

GOLDEN MESH IN CHART FORM

KEY

■ = odd rows

■ = even rows

− = slip stitch

○ = chain

+ = single crochet

Ŧ = double crochet

CROCHETING THE WRAP	
To Begin	Ch 58 loosely.
Row 1	Starting in fourth ch from hook, dc in fourth ch and each ch across, turn (56 dc).
Rows 2 and 3	Ch 3 (counts as dc), dc in each dc across, turn.
Row 4	Ch 5 to turn, ch 6, skip 5 dc, sc in next dc, ch 6, make Trefoil Stitch, ch 6, skip 9 dc, sc in next dc; repeat from * 4 times, ending last repeat sc in top of turning chain, turn.
Row 5	Ch 9 to turn, ch 6, * slip stitch in sc between first and second loop of trefoil, ch 1 behind second loop of trefoil, slip stitch in sc between second and third loop of trefoil, ch 6, make Trefoil Stitch, ch 6; repeat from * 4 times, end sc in top of turning chain, turn.
Row 6	Ch 9 to turn, ch 6, * slip stitch in sc between first and second loop of trefoil, ch 1 in front of second loop of trefoil, slip stitch in sc between second and third loop of trefoil, ch 6, make Trefoil Stitch, ch 6; repeat from * 4 times, sc in top of turning chain, turn.
Row 7	Ch 9 to turn, ch 6, * slip stitch in sc between first and second loop of trefoil, ch 1 behind second loop of trefoil, slip stitch in sc between second and third loop of trefoil, ch 12; repeat from * 4 times, sc in turning chain, turn.
Row 8	Ch 9, sc in first ch-12 space, * ch 9, sc in next ch-12 space; repeat from *, end sc in top of turning chain, turn.
Row 9	Ch 3 (counts as dc), * work 9 dc in ch-9 space, dc in sc; repeat from * across, end 5 dc in last ch-sp, turn (56 dc).
	Repeat Rows 2–9 for stitch pattern until piece measures approximately 60" (152 cm) or 72" (183 cm) from the beginning, end with Row 3 of stitch pattern (3 double crochet rows at the end of the piece). Fasten off.

FINISHING	
	With a large-eye yarn needle, weave in ends.
Blocking	Stretch the lace to the desired dimensions and pin with rust-proof pins. Steam, being careful not to touch the iron to the fabric. You may need to pin out each loop of the trefoils.

Blocking the Trefoils

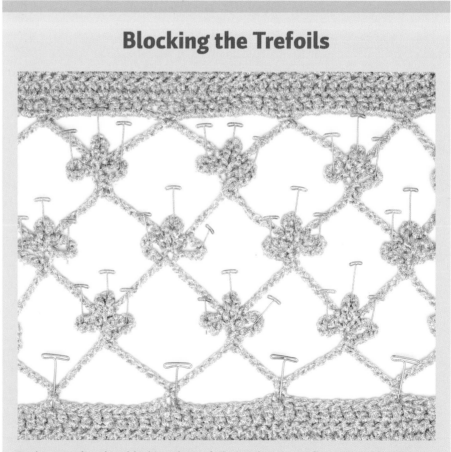

For best results when blocking the trefoils, lay the pins as flat as possible against the pinning surface. This allows you to bring the iron closer to the crochet stitches.

There are many possible ways to wear the Golden Mesh Wrap. This option will display the stitches nicely in both front and back, especially if you wear a solid black blouse or dress underneath.

Meg's Poncho

Designed by Edie Eckman

This stylish poncho is at home in the office or in the carpool. Worked in one piece, it is folded over the shoulder and secured with purchased frog closures. The flirty ruffled edge keeps it from being too severe. The crochet stitches are easy enough for beginners. Try variations on the basic design by adding extra rows for a wider ruffle, adding a few inches of length for a larger size, or using a different edge or closure treatment.

The wool-blend, variegated bouclé yarn creates subtle stripes yet hides any uneven stitches. Experiment with a variety of heavy worsted-weight/bulky-weight yarns to change the look.

Finished measurements
27" (68.5 cm) wide at lower edge × 23" (58 cm) long

Yarn
Heavy worsted to bulky-weight wool or wool-blend bouclé yarn, approximately 78 yds (72 m) per 1.75 oz (50 g) ball in variegated gray

We used Artful Yarns, Legend, 83% wool/17% nylon, 1.75 oz (50 g)/ 78 yds (72 m)
Blackbeard #1493, 6 balls

Crochet hook
One US size H/8 (5 mm), *or size you need to obtain gauge*

Gauge
11½ stitches = 4" in double crochet
Take time to make sure your gauge is correct.

Other supplies
Large-eye yarn needle, four 3½" (9 cm) black frog closures (we used JHB #535)

◆ **ch** = chain stitch ◆ **dc** = double crochet ◆ **sc** = single crochet

CROCHETING THE PONCHO	
To Begin	Ch 43 loosely.
Row 1	Starting in the fourth ch from the hook, dc in fourth chain and each ch across, turn (40 dc). Mark this side as right side.
Row 2	Ch 3 (counts as dc), dc in each dc across, turn.
	Repeat Row 2 until piece measures 24" (61 cm) from beginning, end with a wrong-side row, turn.
Next Row (right side)	Ch 35 (this will take you to corner E as shown in schematic); starting in the fourth ch from hook, dc in fourth ch and each ch across, dc across previous row, turn (72 dc).
Next Row	Ch 3 (counts as dc), dc in each dc across, turn.
Continuing	In double crochet as established, work even in until piece measures 38" (96.5 cm) from the beginning, end with a wrong-side row. (You are at corner A as shown on schematic.) Do not fasten off.
CROCHETING THE EDGING	
Foundation Row	Sc along each edge of piece, working an odd number of stitches on each edge and 3 sc in each of corners B, C, D, E, and A.
Row 1	Beginning at corner A, sc in first stitch, * ch 5, sk 1 sc, sc in next sc **; repeat from * to corner B; ch 6 to turn corner; sc in first stitch on next side; repeat from * to ** to corner C, turn corner as before and continue to corner D, ch 8, turn.
Row 2	* Sc in ch-5 space, ch 5; repeat from * around to corner A. Fasten off.

FINISHING	
	With a large-eye yarn needle, weave in ends.
	Block piece to measurements, following instructions on yarn band.
	Fold poncho as shown along dotted lines (see schematic), over-lapping short and long edge (see photo on page 63). Sew frog closures onto edges, using the photo as a guide.

PONCHO SCHEMATIC

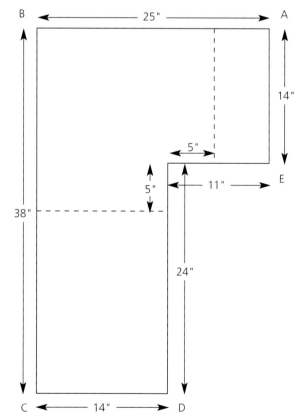

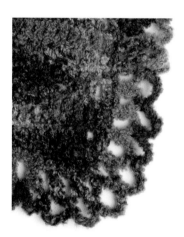

The double row of chain loops along the outside edging gives this poncho an elegant, finished look.

Shirred Scarf

Designed by Edie Eckman

The traditional scarf gets an update with bouncy mohair lace. This scarf *moves* when you do! Ultra-simple lace is knit long, then gathered onto elastic thread for a buoyant, undulating effect. If you prefer, leave off the elastic for a pretty lace scarf.

Although mohair is ideal for this project, you can use any light-weight lofty yarn. Avoid heavy yarn, which will put too much strain on the elastic threads. You can find colored elastic thread at most craft and sewing stores.

Finished measurements
Approximately 10" (25 cm) wide × 44" (112 cm) long after shirring

Yarn
Bulky-weight mohair, mohair-blend, or similar lofty yarn, approximately 90 yds (82 m) per 1.5 oz (42 g) ball in light lime

We used Classic Elite Yarns, La Gran, 76.5% mohair/17.5% wool/6% nylon, 1.5 oz (42 g)/90 yds (82 m) Honeydew #6540, 3 balls

Needles
One pair US size 15 (10 mm), *or size you need to obtain gauge*

Gauge
8 stitches = 4" in Garter Stitch Lace
NOTE: Gauge is not crucial in this project.

Other supplies
8 yds fine weight elastic thread (we used Rainbow Elastic Thread, 50 yds [45 m], size 1 mm Fine in Willow Green #92), large-eye yarn needle

◆ **K** = knit ◆ **K2tog** = knit 2 stitches together ◆ **yo** = yarn over

Garter Stitch Lace

Row 1 * K2, yo, K2tog; repeat from *
across.
    Repeat Row 1 for Garter Stitch Lace.

	KNITTING THE SCARF	
To Begin	Cast on 20 stitches.	
	Work even in Garter Stitch Lace until approximately 36" (90 cm) of yarn remains. Bind off loosely. (Scarf measures approximately 8½ feet [2.6 m] in length.)	
	FINISHING	
	With a large-eye yarn needle, weave in ends.	
Shirring	Cut 6 pieces of elastic each 48" (1.25 m) long.	
	* Thread large-eye yarn needle with 3 strands of elastic. On wrong side, tie elastic onto the second-row stitch of one of the two center solid sections. Weave the elastic through the back of the stitches of every other row of this section to the next-to-last row at the opposite end, gathering fabric as necessary; tie off elastic securely.	
	Repeat from * for other solid center section.	

Threading the Elastic

With a large-eye yarn needle, thread the elastic lengthwise along the scarf through the two innermost bands of K2tog stitches (every other row). Pull both elastic strands evenly to achieve the amount of shirring you prefer.

Snug Fall Cozy

Designed by Jill Wolcott, Y2Knit

This whimsical mini-poncho celebrates the colors of fall. Leaf-patterned bands, accented with beads, create the bottom and neck bands. Clever construction elements make this an intriguing educational exercise. Learn new techniques while you incorporate beads, make integral twisted fringe, and graft small pieces of knitting. Wool yarn is perfect for making twisted fringe because once steamed, it stays put.

Sizes Small, medium, large

Finished measurements
Around shoulders: 40½, 45, 49½" (103, 114, 126 cm)
Length: 7½, 8½, 9½" (19, 21.5, 24 cm), excluding fringe

Yarn
Worsted-weight wool yarn, approximately 245 yds (224 m) per 3.5 oz (100 g) ball in light rust and medium red/brown

> We used Brown Sheep Company, NatureSpun, 100% wool, 3.5 oz (100 g)/245 yds (224 m)
> mc = French Clay #N17; 2, 3, 3 balls
> cc = Burnt Sienna #101, 1 ball all sizes

Needles
US size 10.5 (6.5 mm) circular, 29" long

One pair US size 6 (4 mm) straight
or sizes you need to obtain gauge

Gauge
28 stitches = 4" and 29 rows = 4" in Leaf Pattern using smaller needles
16 stitches = 4" and 20 rows = 4" in Stockinette Stitch using larger needles
Take time to make sure your gauge is correct.

Other supplies
Waste yarn (for provisional cast-on), stitch markers, tapestry needle, 69 (76, 89) beads with holes large enough for yarn

---

◆ **cc** = contrast color ◆ **K** = knit
◆ **K1-f/b, K1-tlb, K3tog,** see Techniques on page 72 ◆ **mc** = main color ◆ **P** = purl ◆ **P1-tbl, sk2p, ssk,** see Techniques on page 72
◆ **yo** = yarn over

TECHNIQUES

K1-f/b = (increase) Knit into the front and back loops of stitch

K1-tbl = (twisted stitch) Knit 1 through the back loop

K3tog = (right-slanting double increase) Knit 3 together

place bead = Bring up bead to piece on right side of fabric. Keeping bead on right side, with yarn in back, slip last stitch worked to left-hand needle, yarn forward, return same stitch to right-hand needle; place yarn into position for next stitch, if necessary.

P1-tbl = (twisted stitch) Purl 1 through the back loop; with yarn in front, insert right-hand needle into the back loop of the next stitch from left to right, purl stitch.

sk2p = Slip 1, knit 2 together, pass slipped stitch over (left-slanting double decrease)

ssk = (single decrease) Slip, slip, knit; slip next 2 stitches, one at a time, as if to knit, to right-hand needle; return stitches to left-hand needle in turned position and K2tog-tbl.

LEAF PATTERN

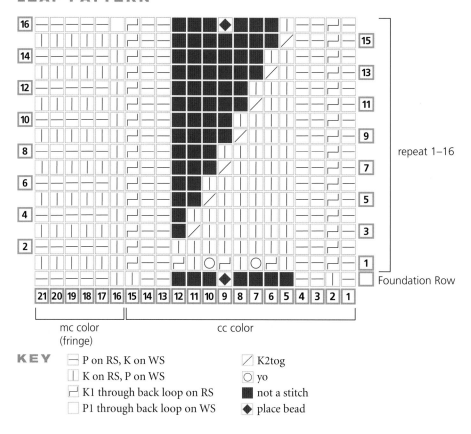

repeat 1–16

mc color
(fringe)

cc color

KEY

⊟ P on RS, K on WS	╱ K2tog
⊔ K on RS, P on WS	○ yo
⌐ K1 through back loop on RS	■ not a stitch
P1 through back loop on WS	◆ place bead

Leaf Pattern (panel of 14 stitches; 16-row repeat)

Foundation Row (wrong side) With mc, K5, P1 (fringe); with cc, P1, K3, place bead, K2, P1, K1 (14 stitches).

Row 1 With cc, P1, K1-tbl, P2, increase 7 stitches in next st by [(K1-f/b, yo) 2 times, K1-f/b], P2, K1-tbl; with mc, K6 (21 sts).

Row 2 With mc, K5, P1; with cc, P1-tbl, K2, P8, K2, P1-tbl, K1.

Row 3 With cc, P1, K1-tbl, P2, K6, K2tog, P2, K1-tbl; with mc, K6 (20 stitches).

Row 4 With mc, K5, P1; with cc, P1-tbl, K2, P7, K2, P1-tbl, K1.

Row 5 With cc, P1, K1-tbl, P2, K5, K2tog, P2, K1-tbl; with mc, K6 (19 stitches).

Row 6 With mc, K5, P1; with cc, P1-tbl, K2, P6, K2, P1-tbl, K1.

Row 7 With cc, P1, K1-tbl, P2, K4, K2tog, P2, K1-tbl; with mc, K6 (18 stitches).

Row 8 With mc, K5, P1; with cc, P1-tbl, K2, P5, K2, P1-tbl, K1.

Row 9 With cc, P1, K1-tbl, P2, K3, K2tog, P2, K1-tbl; with mc, K6 (17 stitches).

Row 10 With mc, K5, P1; with cc, P1-tbl, K2, P4, K2, P1-tbl, K1.

Row 11 With cc, P1, K1-tbl, P2, K2, K2tog, P2, K1-tbl; with mc, K6 (16 stitches).

Row 12 With mc, K5, P1; with cc, P1-tbl, K2, P3, K2, P1-tbl, K1.

Row 13 With cc, P1, K1-tbl, P2, K1, K2tog, P2, K1-tbl; with mc, K6 (15 stitches).

Row 14 With mc, K5, P1; with cc, P1-tbl, K2, P2, K2, P1-tbl, K1.

Row 15 With cc, P1, K1-tbl, P2, K2tog, P2, K1-tbl; with mc, K6 (14 stitches).

Row 16 With mc, K5, P1; with cc, P1-tbl, K2, P1, place bead, K2, P1-tbl, K1.

Repeat Rows 1–16 for Leaf Pattern.

KNITTING THE BOTTOM BAND	SMALL	MEDIUM	LARGE
NOTE: Leave a 12" (30.5 cm) tail of both colors at beginning of band.			
TIP: Leaf Pattern is worked in Intarsia method (using separate balls of yarn for each section). When changing colors, hold the color just worked to the left and pick up the new color from under the old color; this wraps the colors, preventing a hole.			
BEFORE BEGINNING: String ___ beads onto mc.	18	20	22
TO BEGIN: With smaller needles and waste yarn, use the provisional cast-on method (see page 32 or glossary), to cast-on 14 stitches.			
Join mc and cc; work Foundation Row of Leaf Pattern, then work Rows 1–16 a total of ___ times, omitting the bead on the final row.	18	20	22
Cut yarn, leaving an 18" (46 cm) tail of mc.			
With right side facing, using beginning tails, graft 9 stitches of cc and 1 mc stitch (see below) to Foundation Row stitches.			

Grafting Stitches

Grafting is a means of joining live stitches with a threaded needle and yarn for an invisible join. The grafting of the bottom band in this pattern is made stitches to stitches over the waste yarn, which can be removed before or after the graft, as you prefer. Graft purlwise when necessary.

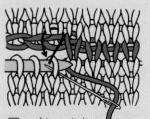

■ grafting stitch
■ provisional cast-on waste yarn

KNITTING THE BODY	SMALL	MEDIUM	LARGE
To Begin: With larger knitting needles and mc, beginning at graft, pick up and knit ___ stitches evenly around top of band between the edge stitch and second stitch.	144	160	176
Setup Round: Place marker for beginning of round, * K ___, pm, K ___, pm, K ___; rep from * once.	7 58 7	8 64 8	9 70 9
Continuing: In stockinette stitch (knit every round), work even until piece measures ___" from bottom band.	2¼	2½	3
NECK AND SHOULDER SHAPING			
Round 1: (Decrease Round 1) * Knit to marker, slip marker, ssk, knit to 2 stitches before next marker, K2tog, slip marker; repeat from * once, knit last ___ stitches.	7	8	9
Round 2: Knit.			
Repeat Rounds 1 and 2 ___ times.	8	9	10
___ stitches remain.	108	120	132
Next Round: (Decrease Round 2) * K ___, slip marker, sk2p, knit to 3 stitches before next marker, K3tog, slip marker, K ___; repeat from * once.	7 7	8 8	9 9
___ stitches remain.	100	112	124
Work Decrease Round 1, then Decrease Round 2 once. ___ stitches remain.	88	100	112
Repeat Decrease Round 1 ___ times.	4	5	6
___ stitches remain.	72	80	88

	SMALL	MEDIUM	LARGE
Knit 2 rounds even.			
Cut yarn, leaving a 2–3 yard (2–3 m) tail. Leave stitches on needles.			
KNITTING THE NECK BAND			
NOTE: Leave a 12" (30.5 cm) tail of mc and cc at beginning of band.			
String ___ beads onto cc and ___ beads onto mc.	9 42	10 46	11 56
Using a provisional cast-on, smaller needles, and waste yarn, cast on 14 stitches.			
Using mc and cc, work the Foundation Row of Leaf Pattern, then work Rows 1–16 ___ times, omitting the bead on the final row.	9	10	11
AT THE SAME TIME, bring a bead to the end of Row 3 and every following fourth row ___ more times, then every other row 6 times and	7	8	9
every fourth row ___ times, then every other row 6 times,	15	17	19
then every fourth row a total of ___ times.	7	8	9
Cut yarn, leaving an 18" (46 cm) tail of mc.			
With right side facing, using the beginning tails, graft beginning to end as for bottom band (see page 74).			

FINISHING (ALL SIZES)

With wrong side facing, graft body stitches to rows of neck-band stitches, skipping cc rows of neck-band. Take care to keep grafted stitches same size as body stitches.

With a large-eye yarn needle, weave in ends, creating extra fringe loops at grafts with tails.

MAKING TWISTED FRINGE

Unravel each mc fringe row (see page 55).

Insert a tapestry needle or small-size double-pointed needle through the end of the fringe loop, twist the needle clockwise until the loop kinks, pull straight, then pin to a blocking surface. Steam several at once to set the twisted yarn.

Block body.

Grafting to Rows

Another way of grafting is from live stitches to finished rows. The principle is the same: use a threaded needle and yarn to create an invisible join. The stitches may not line up exactly with the rows, so skip an occasional row to even things out.

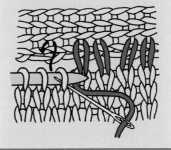

To make the twisted fringe, insert a needle through the end of a loop (second fringe from right, in photo) and turn it like a corkscrew until the yarn kinks up. Then pull it straight and pin it to a blocking surface. Steam several fringes at once to set the twisted yarn.

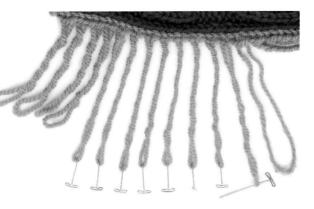

Upcountry Poncho

Designed by Therese Chynoweth

This rustic wrap stirs up images of weekends in the country. Its generous sweep encourages a dramatic entrance — even if it's just into the grocery store. Minimal shaping and one-piece construction appeal to knitters who don't like finishing, while the simple cable and stitch details keep the knitting interesting.

Flecks of color in the tweedy worsted-weight wool add depth to the fabric. You may substitute any worsted-weight yarn, but a color-flecked yarn will look best.

Sizes Small, medium, large

Finished measurements
Width: All sizes, 45" (114 cm)
Length: 25" (63.5 cm), 26½" (67 cm), 28" (71 cm)

Yarn
Heavy worsted-weight wool or wool blend, approximately 108 yds (100 m) per 1.75 oz (50 g) ball in dark brown tweed

We used Lana Grossa, Royal Tweed, 100% merino wool, 1.75 oz (50 g)/ 108 yds (100 m)
#17 (dark brown), 13 (14, 15) balls

Needles
One US size 7 (4.5 mm) circular, 24" (60 cm) long
One US size 8 (5 mm) circular, 32" (80 cm), *or size you need to obtain gauge*

Gauge
15 stitches = 4" and 22 rows = 4" in Stockinette Stitch using larger needle
Take time to make sure your gauge is correct.

Other supplies
Cable needle, large-eye yarn needle, four ¾" buttons, sewing needle, and thread

◆ **K** = knit ◆ **K2tog** = knit 2 stitches together (decrease) ◆ **P** = purl
◆ **yo** = yarn over ◆ **C4B, C4F, C6B,** and **C6F,** see Techniques on page 80

KEY AND TECHNIQUES

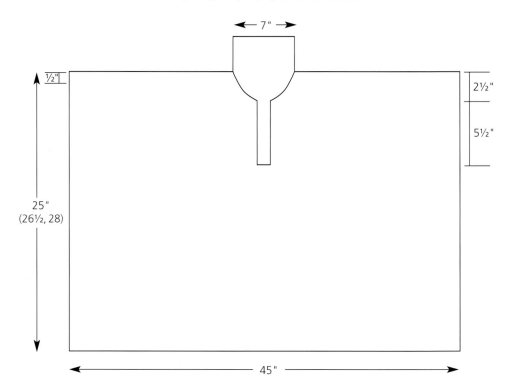

C4B = (4-stitch right-slanting cable) Slip 2 stitches to cable needle and hold in back, K2, K2 from cable needle.

C4F = (4-stitch left-slanting cable) Slip 2 stitches to cable needle and hold in front, K2, K2 from cable needle.

C6B = (6-stitch right-slanting cable) Slip 3 stitches to cable needle and hold in back, K3, K3 from cable needle.

C6F = (6-stitch left-slanting cable) Slip 3 stitches to cable needle and hold in front, K3, K3 from cable needle.

□ K on right side, P on wrong side.

• P on right side, K on wrong side.

+ Edge stitch: slip at beginning of rows and work K on last stitch of right-side rows and P on last stitch of wrong-side rows.

PONCHO SCHEMATIC

← 7" →

½"

2½"

5½"

25"
(26½, 28)

45"

Stitch Patterns

RIB PATTERN
(multiple of 4 plus 1; 2-row repeat)

Row 1 (right side) Slip 1, * P1, K1; repeat from * across.

Row 2 Slip 1, * K3, P1; repeat from * across.

Repeat Rows 1 and 2 for Rib Pattern.

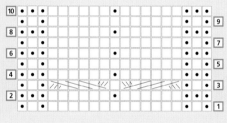

CABLE I
(panel of 19 stitches; 10-row repeat)

Rows 1, 5, 7, and 9 (right side) P1, K1, P1, K13, P1, K1, P1.

Rows 2, 4, 6, 8, and 10 K3, P6, K1, P6, K3.

Row 3 P1, K1, P1, C6B, K1, C6F, P1, K1, P1.

Repeat Rows 1–10 for Cable I.

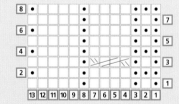

CABLE II (LEFT FRONT PLACKET)
(panel of 13 stitches; 8-row repeat)

Rows 1, 5, and 7 (right side) P1, K1, P1, K4, P1, K5.

Rows 2, 4, 6, and 8 P5, K1, P4, K3.

Row 3 P1, K1, P1, C4B, P1, K5.

Repeat Rows 1–8 for Cable II.

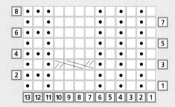

CABLE III (RIGHT FRONT PLACKET)
(panel of 13 stitches; 8-row repeat)

Rows 1, 5, and 7 (right side) (K1, P1) 3 times, K4, P1, K1, P1.

Rows 2, 4, 6, and 8 K3, P4, (K1, P1) 3 times.

Row 3 (K1, P1) 3 times, C4F, P1, K1, P1.

Repeat Rows 1–8 for Cable III.

KNITTING THE PONCHO	SMALL	MEDIUM	LARGE
NOTE: Poncho is worked back and forth on circular needles to accommodate the large number of stitches, beginning at lower edge of front, working over shoulders to lower edge of back.			
NOTE: Work Edge Stitches as follows: Slip the first stitch of every row; knit the last stitch on right-side rows, purl the last stitch on wrong-side rows.			
To BEGIN: With larger needle, cast on 189 stitches.			
Rows 1–10: Work Rows 1 and 2 of Rib Pattern 5 times, working Edge Stitches each row as noted above. Rib measures approximately 1¾" (4.5 cm) from beginning.			
Row 11 (setup): Work 6 sts in Rib Pattern as established, K15, beginning Row 1 of Cable I, * work Cable I across 19 stitches, K45, repeat from * once, work Cable I across 19 stitches, K15, work remaining 6 stitches in Rib Pattern as established.			
Row 12: Work 6 sts in Rib Pattern as established, P15, * continue Cable I as established across 19 stitches, P14, place marker, K1, P15, place marker, K1, P14; repeat from * once, continue Cable I as established across 19 stitches, P15, work remaining 6 stitches in Rib Pattern as established.			
Work even in patterns as established, and slipping markers as you come to them, until poncho measures approximately ___ from beginning, end with (wrong side) Row 6 of Cable I.	17" (43 cm)	18½" (47 cm)	20" (50.8 cm)

DIVIDE FOR NECK	SMALL	MEDIUM	LARGE
Row 1 (left front): Work 85 stitches as established, P1, K1, P1, K4, cast on 6 stitches for button placket (98 stitches for left neck).			
Continuing Row 1 (right front): Attach a second ball of yarn, K1, (P1, K1) twice, increase 1 stitch for buttonhole placket, K4, P1, K1, P1, then work remaining stitches as established (98 stitches for right neck).			
Row 2 (right front): Work 85 stitches as established, work Row 2 of Cable III over next 13 stitches.			
Row 2 (left front): Work Row 2 of Cable Pattern II over next 13 stitches, work remaining 85 stitches as established.			
Next Rows: Work both sides at the same time as established, and AT THE SAME TIME, when placket measures 1" (2.5 cm) from dividing row, end with a wrong-side row. Work across left front as established; on right front, work buttonhole as follows: K1, P1, K1, yo, K2tog, work as established to end.			
Continue to work even as established, working 2 additional buttonholes every 12 rows, until poncho measures approximately _____ from beginning.	22½" (57 cm)	24" (61 cm)	25½" (64.7 cm)
SHAPING THE FRONT NECK			
Bind off 9 stitches at each neck edge once, then bind off 2 stitches once (87 stitches remain on each side).			

	SMALL	MEDIUM	LARGE
Continuing to work in pattern, decrease 1 stitch at each neck edge every other row 5 times (82 stitches remain on each side).			
Work even until poncho measures approximately ____ from beginning. Work 1 more row.	25" (63.5 cm)	26½" (67 cm)	28" (71 cm)
SHAPING THE BACK NECK			
Cast on 2 stitches at each neck edge twice (86 stitches each side).			
Work half of body as established, cast on 17 stitches, work remaining half of body (189 stitches).			
Next Row: Work first 85 stitches as established, work Cable Pattern I (same row as worked on sides) across next 19 stitches, work remaining 85 stitches in established pattern.			
Work even as established until piece measures approximately ____ from beginning, end with a right-side row.	48¼" (123 cm)	51¼" (130 cm)	54¼" (137.75 cm)
Work 10 rows in Rib Pattern as for front, end with a right-side row. Bind off all stitches loosely in pattern.			

FINISHING	SMALL	MEDIUM	LARGE
With large-eye yarn needle, weave in ends.			
Block poncho to measurements.			
Sew cast-on edge of button placket (left front) to wrong side under buttonhole placket.			
COLLAR			
Using smaller circular needle, pick up and knit 73 stitches along neck edge.			
Work back and forth, working button placket in Stockinette Stitch and buttonhole placket in K1, P1 rib as established, and lining up ribs on each side of cables. AT THE SAME TIME, work remaining buttonhole 12 rows above third buttonhole.			
Bind off all stitches loosely in pattern.			
Sew buttons to button placket under buttonholes.			

Starlet Shrug

Designed by Kathleen Power Johnson

You'll feel like a movie star in this shapely crocheted shrug. Luxurious hand-painted yarn feels yummy against your skin. The highly textured stitch pattern is perfect for the subtly variegated yarn. The merino wool is so velvety soft, it feels like cotton — or substitute any smooth worsted-weight yarn and eyelash-style novelty yarn. Shaping and stitch patterning maintain the interest of intermediate and advanced crocheters.

Sizes Small, medium, large

Finished measurements

Bust: 36" (91.5 cm), 40" (101.5 cm), 44" (111.7 cm)

Back length: 12½" (31.75 cm), 13" (33 cm), 13½" (34.25 cm)

NOTE: This shrug fits snugly and is not meant to meet at the center front.

Yarn

Worsted-weight wool or wool-blend yarn, 188 yds (172 m) per 3.5 oz (100 g) skein; bulky-weight novelty silk-blend yarn, 48 yds (43 m) per .8 oz (25 g) skein

We used Artyarns, UltraMerino 8, 100% merino wool, hand-painted, 3.5 oz (100 g)/188 yds (172 m) mc = #115 (red multi), 4 (4, 5) skeins *and* Artyarns, Silk Fur, 90% silk,

10% nylon, .8 oz (25 g)/48 yds (43 m) cc = #115 (red multi), 1 skein

Crochet hooks

One US size 7 (4.5 mm), One US size M-N/13 (9 mm), *or sizes you need to obtain gauge*

Gauge

16 stitches = 4" and 8 rows = 4" in Crossed Stitch pattern. NOTE: Row gauge is important in this pattern. Do your best to match both stitch and row gauges.

Other supplies

Large-eye yarn needle

◆ **ch** = chain ◆ **dc** = double crochet ◆ **hdc** = half double crochet ◆ **LC, RC,** see Techniques on page 88 ◆ **sc** = single crochet

Crossed Stitch Pattern

Use instructions below for checking your gauge (multiple of 3 stitches plus 2; 2-row repeat).

Row 1 (wrong side) Starting in second ch from hook, sc in back loop only of second ch and each ch across, turn.

Row 2 Ch 3 (counts as dc), skip first stitch, work LC across to last stitch, end dc in last stitch, turn.

Row 3 Ch 3 (counts as dc), skip first stitch, work RC across to last stitch, end dc in top of turning chain, turn.

Row 4 Ch 3 (counts as dc), LC across to last stitch, dc in top of turning chain, turn.

Repeat Rows 3 and 4 for Crossed Stitch Pattern.

TECHNIQUES

LC = (left cross) Skip 1 stitch, inserting hook from front to back, double crochet in each of next 2 stitches, dc in skipped stitch.

RC = (right cross) Skip 1 stitch, inserting hook from back to front, double crochet in each of next 2 stitches, inserting hook behind 2 dc last made; double crochet loosely in skipped stitch.

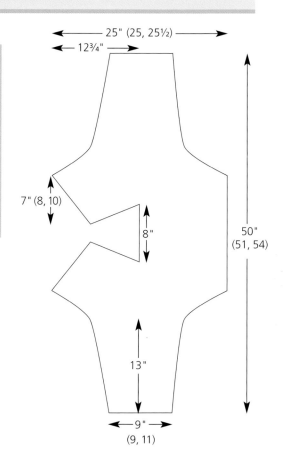

CROCHETING THE SHRUG *Left Sleeve*	SMALL	MEDIUM	LARGE
NOTE 1: Chain 3 counts as a double crochet throughout.			
NOTE 2: When increasing, maintain pattern stitch by adding one pattern repeat for every 3 increased stitches.			
NOTE 3: Some rows will not contain complete pattern repeats. On these rows, double crochet in each of the remaining stitches. Maintain at least 1 dc stitch on either side of the Crossed Stitch groups.			
TO BEGIN: With smaller hook and mc, ch ____.	39	39	45
Row 1 (wrong side): Work Row 1 of Crossed Stitch Pattern, turn. (____ stitches)	38	38	44
Row 2: Work Row 2 of Crossed Stitch Pattern, turn. (____ left crosses)	12	12	14
Row 3: Work Row 3 of Crossed Stitch Pattern, turn. (____ right crosses)	12	12	14
Row 4: Ch 3, dc in base of turning chain (1 stitch increased), LC ____ times across, end dc in last dc (1 stitch increased), dc in top of turning chain, turn.	12	12	14
Row 5: Ch 3, dc in first dc, RC ____ times across, end dc in last dc, dc in top of turning chain, turn.	12	12	14
Continuing: Work in Crossed Stitch Pattern as established, increasing 1 stitch each side every fourth row ____ more time(s), then every other row ____ times. (____ stitches)	2 7 58	1 9 60	1 9 66

SHAPING THE BODY	SMALL	MEDIUM	LARGE
Row 1 (wrong side): Work in pattern as established, end ch 8, turn.			
Row 2: Starting in fourth ch from hook, dc in fourth ch, and next _____ chain, LC across, end dc in each of last _____ dc, ch 8, turn. (_____ stitches, excluding chain)	0 2 64	1 3 66	1 3 72
Row 3: Starting in fourth ch from hook, dc in fourth ch and next _____ chain, RC across, end dc in each of last _____ dc, ch _____, turn. (_____ stitches, excluding chain)	0 2 18 70	1 3 17 72	1 3 15 78
Row 4: Starting in fourth ch from hook, dc in fourth ch and next _____ chain(s), LC across, end dc in last _____ dc, ch _____, turn. (_____ stitches, excluding chain)	1 1 18 86	1 3 17 87	2 3 15 91
Row 5: Starting in fourth ch from hook, dc in fourth ch and next _____ chain(s), RC across, end dc in last _____ dc, turn. (_____ stitches)	1 3 102	1 3 102	2 1 104
Row 6: Work even in established pattern, turn. For next rows, go to the appropriate size on the next page.			
NOTE: For all sizes, when working slip stitches at beginning of rows, the chain-3 counts as a stitch. It sits directly above the final slipped stitch. Work the next stitch in pattern into the next stitch on the row.			

For Size Small

Rows 7, 9, 11, 13: Slip stitch in first 3 stitches, ch 3, work in pattern to end, turn.

Rows 8, 10, 12: Ch 3, work in pattern to end, turn.

Row 14: Ch 3, work in pattern over next 50 stitches, place marker, work to end of row, turn (51 stitches for back, 43 stitches for front).

Skip to *Left Front Neck Shaping.*

For Size Medium

Rows 7, 9, 11: Slip stitch in first 3 stitches, ch 3, work in pattern to end, turn.

Rows 8, 10, 12: Ch 3, work in pattern to end, turn.

Rows 13, 15: Slip stitch in first 2 stitches, ch 3, work in pattern to end, turn.

Row 14: Ch 3, work in pattern to end, turn.

Row 16: Ch 3, work in pattern over 50 stitches, place marker, work to end, turn. (51 stitches for back, 43 stitches for front)

Skip to *Left Front Neck Shaping.*

For Size Large

Rows 7, 9, 11: Slip stitch in first 3 stitches, ch 3, work in pattern to end, turn.

Rows 8, 10, 12: Ch 3, work in pattern to end, turn.

Rows 13, 15, 17: Slip stitch in first 2 stitches, ch 3, work in pattern to end, turn.

Rows 14, 16: Ch 3, work in pattern to end, turn.

Row 18: Ch 3, work in pattern over 51 stitches, place marker, work to end, turn (52 stitches for back, 43 stitches for front).

LEFT FRONT NECK SHAPING (All Sizes)	SMALL	MEDIUM	LARGE
Row ____: Slip stitch in first 2 stitches, ch 3, work in pattern to last 6 stitches, turn (36 stitches remain).	15	17	19
Row ____: Slip stitch in first 7 stitches, ch 3, work in pattern to end, turn (30 stitches remain).	16	18	20
Row ____: Slip stitch in first 2 stitches, ch 3, work in pattern to last 6 stitches, turn (23 stitches remain).	17	19	21
Row ____: Slip stitch in first 7 stitches, ch 3, work in pattern to end, turn (17 stitches remain).	18	20	22
Row ____: Slip stitch in first 2 stitches, ch 3, work in pattern to last 6 stitches, turn (10 stitches remain).	19	21	23
Row ____: Slip stitch in first 6 stitches, ch 3, LC, dc in turning chain, turn (5 stitches remain).	20	22	24
Row____: Ch 2, RC, ch 1, slip stitch into next stitch. Fasten off.	21	23	25
BACK AND RIGHT FRONT			
Join yarn to marked stitch at neckline (____ stitches).	51	51	52
Row 1 (wrong side): Ch 3, work in established pattern to end, turn.			
Row 2: Ch 3, work in pattern to last 3 stitches, turn (____ stitches remain).	48	48	49
Rows 3–13: Work even in pattern.			

	SMALL	MEDIUM	LARGE
Row 14: Ch 3, work in pattern across, end ch 5, turn.			
Row 15: Dc in fourth ch from hook, work in pattern across, turn (_____ stitches).	51	51	52
Row 16: Ch 3, work in pattern across, end ch 45 for front, turn.			
Row 17: Dc in fourth ch from hook and next 2 ch, RC across, end dc in turning chain, turn (_____ stitches). For next rows, go to appropriate size below.	94	94	95

For Size Small

Row 18: Ch 3, work in pattern across, ch 4, turn.

Row 19: Dc in fourth ch from hook, work in pattern to end, turn (96 stitches).

Row 20: Ch 3, work in pattern across, ch 4, turn.

Row 21: Dc in fourth ch from hook, work in pattern to end, turn (98 stitches).

Row 22: Ch 3, work in pattern across, ch 4, turn.

Row 23: Dc in fourth ch from hook, work in pattern to end, turn (100 stitches).

Row 24: Ch 3, work in pattern across, ch 4, turn.

Row 25: Dc in fourth ch from hook, work in pattern to end, turn (102 stitches).

Skip to *For All Sizes*.

For Size Medium

Row 18: Ch 3, work in pattern across, ch 2, turn.

Row 19: Dc in first stitch, work in pattern to end, turn (95 stitches).

Row 20: Ch 3, work in pattern across, ch 2, turn.

Row 21: Dc in first stitch, work in pattern to end, turn (96 stitches).

Row 22: Ch 3, work in pattern across, ch 4, turn.

Row 23: Dc in fourth ch from hook, work in pattern to end, turn (98 stitches).

Row 24: Ch 3, work in pattern across, ch 4, turn.

Row 25: Dc in fourth ch from hook, work in pattern to end, turn (100 stitches).

Row 26: Ch 3, work in pattern across, ch 4, turn.

Row 27: Dc in fourth ch from hook, work in pattern to end, turn (102 stitches).

Skip to *For All Sizes.*

For Size Large

Row 18: Ch 3, work in pattern across, ch 2, turn.

Row 19: Dc in first stitch, work in pattern to end, turn (96 stitches).

Row 20: Ch 3, work in pattern across, ch 2, turn.

Row 21: Dc in first stitch, work in pattern to end, turn (97 stitches).

Row 22: Ch 3, work in pattern across, ch 2, turn.

Row 23: Dc in first stitch, work in pattern to end, turn (98 stitches).

Row 24: Ch 3, work in pattern across, ch 4, turn.

Row 25: Dc in fourth ch from hook, work in pattern to end, turn (100 stitches).

Row 26: Ch 3, work in pattern across, ch 4, turn.

Row 27: Dc in fourth ch from hook, work in pattern to end, turn (102 stitches).

Row 28: Ch 3, work in pattern across, ch 4, turn.

Row 29: Dc in fourth ch from hook, work in pattern to end, turn (104 stitches).

For All Sizes	SMALL	MEDIUM	LARGE
Row ____: Ch 3, work in pattern across, turn.	26	28	30
Row ____: Slip stitch across ____ stitches, ch 3, work in pattern to end, turn.	27 17	29 16	31 14
____ stitches remain.	86	87	91
Row ____: Slip stitch across ____ stitches, ch 3, work in pattern to end, turn.	28 17	30 16	32 14
____ stitches remain.	70	72	78
Row ____: Slip stitch across 7 stitches, ch 3, work in pattern to end, turn.	29	31	33
____ stitches remain.	64	66	72
Row ____: Slip stitch across 7 stitches, ch 3, work in pattern to end, turn.	30	32	34
____ stitches remain.	58	60	66
RIGHT SLEEVE			
Ch 3, work in pattern to end, turn.			
Working in pattern as established, decrease each side of every RS row ____ times, then each side of every fourth row ____ times (____ stitches remain).	7 3 38	9 2 38	9 2 44
Work 2 rows even in pattern.			
Chain 1, sc across. Fasten off.			
RIGHT FRONT NECK SHAPING			
With right side facing, join yarn to lower front edge.			

	SMALL	MEDIUM	LARGE
Row 1: Ch 1, slip stitch across 2 stitches, ch 3, work next 35 stitches in pattern, turn (36 stitches remain).			
Row 2: Slip stitch across 7 stitches, ch 3, work next 29 stitches in pattern, turn (30 stitches remain).			
Row 3: Slip stitch across 2 stitches, ch 3, work next 22 stitches in pattern, turn (23 stitches remain).			
Row 4: Slip stitch across 7 stitches, ch 3, work next 16 stitches in pattern, turn (17 stitches remain).			
Row 5: Slip stitch across 2 stitches, ch 3, work next 9 stitches in pattern, turn (10 stitches remain).			
Row 6: Slip stitch across 6 stitches, ch 3, work next 4 stitches in pattern, turn (5 stitches remain).			
Row 7: Ch 2, LC, ch 1, slip stitch into next stitch. Fasten off.			
CROCHETING THE COLLAR			
Sew underarm seams.			
Join cc at lower corner of right front.			
Row 1: With right side facing and larger hook, ch 2 (counts as hdc), hdc into edge around neckline to left front corner, turn.			
Row 2: Ch 2, hdc in next 3 stitches, dc to within last 3 stitches, hdc in last 3 stitches, hdc around turning ch, turn.			

	SMALL	MEDIUM	LARGE
Row 3: Ch 1, sc in next 3 stitches, hdc in next 3 stitches, dc to within last 6 stitches, 3 hdc, 3 sc, sc around turning ch, turn.			
Row 4: Slip stitch into first 3 stitches, sc into next 3 stitches, hdc into next 3 stitches, dc to within the last 9 stitches, hdc into next 3 stitches, sc into next 3 stitches, slip stitch into next stitch, turn.			
Row 5: Slip stitch into first 3 stitches, sc into next 3 stitches, hdc in next 3 stitches, dc to last 9 dc, hdc in 3 dc, sc in next 3 stitches, slip stitch in next stitch. Fasten off.			
With mc, leaving a 10" (25.5 cm) tail of yarn at each end, work slip stitch from front point of right front, along edge of back, and to front point of left front. Fold back collar against fronts and use yarn tails to tack in place at lower edge.			

To crochet the collar onto the shrug, start at the right front (lower corner), then work up and around the neckline and down the left front. Fold the completed collar back and tack it in place at each front corner.

Aran Poncho

Designed by Therese Chynoweth

Everything old is new again in this dramatic update on the traditional Aran sweater. Details tell the story here. A mix of lovely stitch patterns on two straight panels makes up the body of the poncho. The patterns on the yoke are designed to flow seamlessly from one to another. Whether you make the large-collar version (shown) or the optional short collar, this is a design that is as satisfying to knit as it is to wear.

Finished measurements
37" (94 cm) wide × 31" (78.75 cm) long from shoulder to lower edge; yoke approximately 14¾" (37.5 cm) wide

Yarn
Worsted-weight wool or wool blend, approximately 88 yds (80 m) per 1.75 oz (50 g) ball in natural

We used Dale of Norway, Free Style, 100% pure new wool, 1.75 oz (50 g), 88 yds (80 m), #0020 (natural), 14 balls for short-collar version (15 balls for large-collar version)

Needle
One US size 7 (4.5 mm) circular, 24" (60 cm) long, *or size you need to obtain gauge*

Gauge
16 stitches = 4" and 22 rows = 4" in Stockinette Stitch
Take time to make sure your gauge is correct.

Other supplies
Large-eye yarn needle, two stitch markers, stitch holders, or waste yarn

> ◆ **K** = knit ◆ **K2tog** = knit 2 stitches together (single decrease) ◆ **K3tog** = knit 3 stitches together (double decrease) ◆ **M1** = make 1 (increase) ◆ **P** = purl ◆ **P3tog** = purl 3 stitches together (double decrease) ◆ **ssk** = slip, slip, knit (single decrease) ◆ **T2L, T2R** (Techniques, page 100) ◆ **yo** = yarn over

Stitch Patterns

KEY AND TECHNIQUES

◻ K on RS, P on WS

• P on RS, K on WS

⬓ **C2L** = (cross 2 left) Knit into back of second stitch on left-hand needle, do not remove stitch from needle, knit first stitch, drop both stitches off left-hand needle.

⬔ **C2R** = (cross 2 right) Knit into front of second stitch on left-hand needle, do not remove stitch from needle, knit first stitch, drop both stitches off left-hand needle.

⬔ **T2L** = (twist 2 left) Purl into back of second stitch on left-hand needle, do not remove stitch from needle, knit first stitch, drop both stitches off left-hand needle.

⬔ **T2R** = (twist 2 right) Knit into front of second stitch on left-hand needle, do not remove stitch from needle, purl first stitch, drop both stitches off left-hand needle.

○ yarn over

⟍ ssk (slip, slip, knit)

⟋ K2tog (knit 2 together)

PATTERN I
(multiple of 10 stitches plus 5; 6-row repeat)

Row 1 (wrong side): K2 (edge stitches), * P1, K3, P3, K3; repeat from * to last 3 stitches, end P1, K2 (edge stitches).

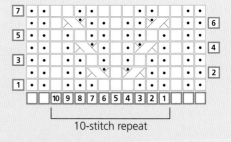

10-stitch repeat

Row 2: P2 (edge stitches), K1, * P2, T2R, K1, T2L, P2, K1; repeat from * to last 2 stitches, end P2 (edge stitches).

Row 3: K2, * P1, K2, [P1, K1] twice, P1, K2; repeat from * to last 3 stitches, end P1, K2.

Row 4: P2, K1, * P1, T2R, P1, K1, P1, T2L, P1, K1, repeat from * to last 2 stitches, end P2.

Row 5: K2, * P1, K1, [P1, K2] twice, P1, K1; repeat from * to last 3 stitches, end P1, K2.

Row 6: P2, K1, * T2R, P2, K1, P2, T2L, K1; repeat from * to last 2 stitches, end P2.

Row 7: K2, * P2, K2, P3, K2, P1; rep from * to last 3 sts, end, P1, K2.

Repeat Rows 2–7 for Pattern 1.

ARAN PATTERN LEFT
(20 stitches; 6-row repeat)

Rows 1, 3, 5 (wrong side): K2, P1, K2, P6, K2, P1, K2, P2, K2.

Row 2: P2, C2R, P2, K1, P2, K2, K2tog, K2, yo, P2, K1, P2.

Row 4: P2, C2R, [P2, K1] twice, K2tog, K2, yo, [K1, P2] twice.

Row 6: P2, C2R, P2, K1, P2, K2tog, K2, yo, K2, P2, K1, P2.

Repeat Rows 1–6 for Aran Left.

ARAN PATTERN CENTER
(26 stitches; 30-row repeat)

Row 1 (wrong side): P1, K11, P2, K11, P1.

Row 2: K1, P8, [C2R, P1] twice, C2R, P8, K1.

Row 3: P1, K8, [P2, K1] twice, P2, K8, P1.

Row 4: K1, P7, T2R, K1, P1, C2R, P1, K1, T2L, P7, K1.

Row 5: P1, K7, [P1, K1] twice, P2, [K1, P1] twice, K7, P1.

Row 6: K1, P6, T2R, [C2R, P1] twice, C2L, T2L, P6, K1.

Row 7: P1, K6, P1, [K1, P2] 3 times, K1, P1, K6, P1.

Row 8: K1, P5, T2R twice, K1, P1, C2R, P1, K1, T2L twice, P5, K1.

Row 9: P1, K5, [P1, K1] 3 times, P2, [K1, P1] 3 times, K5, P1.

(continued on next page)

Stitch Patterns (continued)

Row 10: K1, P4, T2R twice, [C2R, P1] twice, C2L, T2L twice, P4, K1.
Row 11: P1, K4, [P1, K1] twice, [P2, K1] 3 times, P1, K1, P1, K4, P1.
Row 12: K1, P3, T2R 3 times, K1, P1, C2R, P1, K1, T2L 3 times, P3, K1.
Row 13: P1, K3, [P1, K1] 4 times, P2, [K1, P1] 4 times, K3, P1.
Row 14: K1, P2, T2R 3 times, [C2R, P1] twice, C2L, T2L 3 times, P2, K1.
Row 15: P1, K4, [P1, K1] twice, [P2, K1] 3 times, [P1, K1] twice, K3, P1.
Row 16: K1, P3, T2R 3 times, K1, P1, C2R, P1, K1, T2L 3 times, P3, K1.
Row 17: P1, K5, [P1, K1] 3 times, P2, [K1, P1] 3 times, K5, P1.
Row 18: K1, P4, T2R twice, [C2R, P1] twice, C2L, T2L twice, P4, K1.
Row 19: P1, K6, P1, [K1, P2] 3 times, K1, P1, K6, P1.
Row 20: K1, P5, T2R twice, K1, P1, C2R, P1, K1, T2L twice, P5, K1.
Row 21: P1, K7, [P1, K1] twice, P2, [K1, P1] twice, K7, P1.
Row 22: K1, P6, T2R, [C2R, P1] twice, C2L, T2L, P6, K1.
Row 23: P1, K8, [P2, K1] twice, P2, K8, P1.
Row 24: K1, P7, T2R, K1, P1, C2R, P1, K1, T2L, P7, K1.
Row 25: P1, K9, P1, K1, P2, K1, P1, K9, P1.
Row 26: K1, P8, [C2R, P1] twice, C2L, P8, K1.
Row 27: Repeat Row 25.
Row 28: K1, P9, K1, P1, C2R, P1, K1, P9, K1.
Row 29: P1, K11, P2, K11, P1.
Row 30: K1, P11, C2R, P11, K1.
Repeat Rows 1–30 for Aran Center.

ARAN PATTERN RIGHT
(20 stitches; 6-row repeat)
Rows 1, 3, 5 (wrong side): K2, P2, K2, P1, K2, P6, K2, P1, K2.
Row 2: P2, K1, P2, yo, K2, ssk, K2, P2, K1, P2, C2R, P2.
Row 4: [P2, K1] twice, yo, K2, ssk, [K1, P2] twice, C2R, P2.
Row 6: P2, K1, P2, K2, yo, K2, ssk, P2, K1, P2, C2R, P2.
Repeat Rows 1–6 for Aran Right.

[Knitting chart: 20 stitches wide (numbered 20–1), 6 rows (numbered 1–6).]

SIDE EDGE PATTERN
(multiple of 10 stitches plus 3; 6 rows)

Row 1 (wrong side): K1, * P1, K3, P3, K3; repeat from * to last 2 stitches, end P1, K1.

Row 2: P1, K1, * P2, T2R, K1, T2L, P2, K1; repeat from * to last stitch, end P1.

Row 3: K1, * P1, K2, [P1, K1] twice, P1, K2; repeat from * to last 2 stitches, end P1, K1.

Row 4: P1, K1, * P1, T2R, P1, K1, P1, T2L, P1, K1; repeat from * to last stitch, end P1.

Row 5: K1, * P1, K1, [P1, K2] twice, P1, K1; repeat from * to last 2 stitches, end P1, K1.

Row 6: P1, K1, * T2R, P2, K1, P2, T2L, K1; repeat from * to last stitch, end P1.

Repeat Rows 1–6 for Side Edges.

10-stitch repeat

YOKE PATTERN (IN THE ROUND)
(multiple of 10 stitches; 6-round repeat)

Round 1: P2, T2R, K1, T2L, P2, K1.

Round 2: P2, [K1, P1] twice, K1, P2, K1.

Round 3: P1, T2R, P1, K1, P1, T2L, P1, K1.

Round 4: P1, K1, P2, K1, P2, K1, P1, K1.

Round 5: T2R, P2, K1, P2, T2L, K1.

Round 6: K1, P2, K3, P2, K2.

Repeat Rounds 1–6 for Yoke Pattern.

COLLAR PATTERN
(multiple of 8 stitches plus 3)

Row 1: K2, * T2L, P1, K1, P1, T2R, K1; repeat from * to last 5 stitches, end T2L, P1 K2.

Row 2: P2, K1, P1, K1, * (P1, K1) 4 times; repeat from * to last 2 stitches, end P2.

Row 3: K2, * P1, T2L, K1, T2R, P1, K1; repeat from * to last 5 stitches, end P1, T2L, K2.

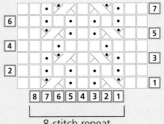

8-stitch repeat

Row 4: P3, K1, P1, * P2, K1, P3, K1, P1; repeat from * to last 2 stitches, end P2.

Row 5: K2, * T2L, P1, K1, P1, T2R, K1; repeat from * to last 5 stitches, end T2L, P1, K2.

Row 6: P2, K1, P1, K1, * (P1, K1) four times; repeat from * to last 2 stitches, end P2.

Row 7: K2, * P1, T2L, K1, T2R, P1, K1; repeat from * to last 5 stitches, end P1, T2L, K2.

PONCHO SCHEMATIC

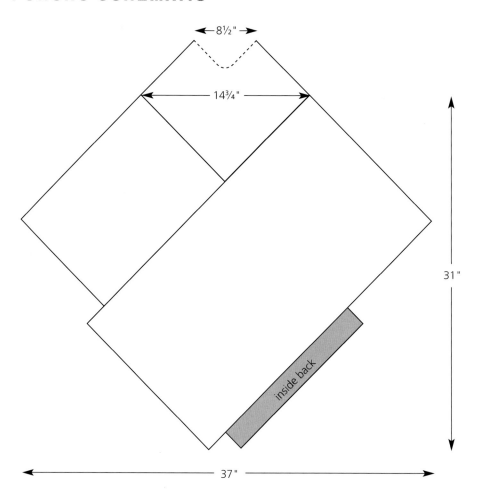

KNITTING THE PANELS (MAKE 2)	
To Begin	Cast on 65 stitches.
	Starting with Row 1 (wrong side) and working back and forth on a circular needle, work 2 repeats of Pattern 1. On the last row, increase 1 stitch at the center. You now have 66 stitches.
Note	You begin all wrong-side rows with Aran Pattern Left and all right-side rows with Aran Pattern Right. Place markers to set off the two 20-stitch side patterns from the 26-stitch center pattern.
Next Row (wrong side)	Work the 20 stitches of Aran Pattern Left, the 26 stitches of Aran Pattern Center, and the 20 stitches of Aran Pattern Right. Note: If you are following the charts, read Row 1 of the charts from left to right, beginning at the bottom left.
Next Rows	Continue in established patterns, repeating the 6 rows of Aran Patterns Left and Right 35 times and the 30 rows of Aran Pattern Center 7 times. End last repeat with Row 28 of Aran Pattern Center. Panel measures approximately 40" (1 m) from beginning.
	Bind off all stitches loosely in pattern.

KNITTED PANEL

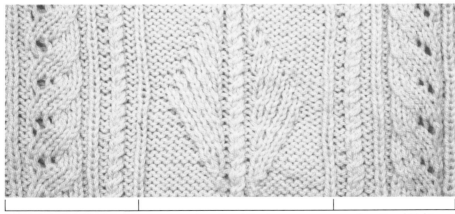

| Aran Panel Left | Aran Panel Center | Aran Panel Right |

Right Side Edge	With right side facing, pick up and knit 193 stitches along right-hand edge of panel. TIP: This is not quite 1 stitch per row. Divide the piece into equal parts to help estimate the pickup.
Next Rows	Beginning on the wrong side, work the 6 rows of the Side Edge Pattern.
Bind Off	With wrong side facing, knit and bind off 9 stitches (10 stitches worked), * slip next 2 stitches together to right-hand needle purl-wise through back loops, return slipped stitches to left-hand needle in turned position, K3tog (double decrease), bind off that stitch, then bind off the next 7 stitches; repeat from * to end. NOTE: You are working double decreases over the 3 stitches that form the inverted V (stitches 1, 10, and 9 of the pattern); this technique makes a smoother edge.
Left Side Edge	Work as for Right Side Edge for 6 rows.
Binding off	With wrong side facing, bind off the first 101 stitches as for Right Side, then work Row 1 of Side Edge Pattern across remaining 92 stitches. Thread yarn needle with waste yarn and draw it through the remaining stitches; set aside.
	Make second panel to match.
FINISHING THE PANELS	
	With large-eye yarn needle, weave in all ends.
	Block both panels to 17" (43 cm) × 40" (101.5 cm). NOTE: Panels will relax to approximately 16" (40.5 cm) wide.
ASSEMBLING THE PANELS	
	Sew bottom (short) bound-off end of one panel to bound-off portion of left edge of second panel, placing live stitches on waste yarn next to each other and right edge approximately 2" (5 cm) from lower end of second panel. Sew bound-off end of second panel to bound-off portion of left edge of first panel in same manner. (See diagram on next page.)

PANEL (MAKE 2)

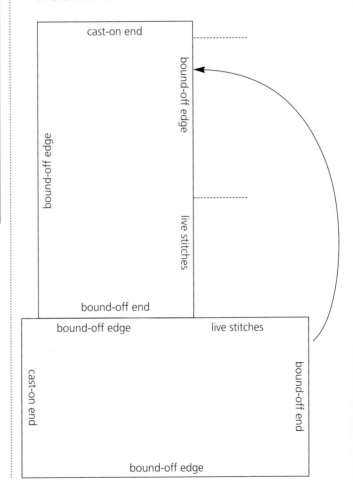

bound-off end

live stitches

bound-off edge

bound-off edge

cast-on end

ASSEMBLY

cast-on end

bound-off edge

bound-off edge

live stitches

bound-off end

bound-off edge

live stitches

cast-on end

bound-off end

bound-off edge

KNITTING THE YOKE

To Begin	Place live stitches from waste yarn on both panels onto needle. You now have 184 stitches. Join yarn where pieces meet at front. Place a marker at this point to mark the beginning of round (center front); place a second marker where pieces meet at back (between stitches 92 and 93). Yoke is worked in the round on a circular needle. (NOTE: Be sure to work the chart from right to left on each round.) Work Yoke Pattern, keeping pattern as established for side edge, and AT THE SAME TIME work decreases at the center front and center back, as follows:
Round 1 (right side)	K2tog, work Round 1 of Yoke Pattern to marker at center back, slip marker, K2tog, work in pattern to end of round. You now have 182 stitches.
Round 2	* Ssk, work Round 2 of pattern to 2 stitches before marker, K2tog, slip marker; repeat from * to end of round. You now have 178 stitches.
Next Round	Work even in pattern as established.
Next Rounds	Continue to work the 6 pattern lines as established, decreasing 4 stitches every other round as in Round 2 ten more times. End with Round 5 of pattern. You now have 138 stitches.
Next Round	Continuing in the pattern, decrease 4 stitches as before every round 3 times. End with Round 2 of pattern. You now have 126 stitches.
Dividing for collar	Work even on Round 3; turn. NOTE: This marks the beginning of the collar. You will be working back and forth in rows from here to the end.
Next Row (right side)	Working Row 4 of pattern, decrease 1 stitch on each side of center back marker.
Next Row	Work even in pattern as established.
Next Row	Working Row 6 of pattern, K2tog at center back. You now have 123 stitches.

Decrease Row (wrong side)	Work 5 stitches in pattern as established, * slip 1 purlwise, slip 1 knitwise, insert left needle from right to left into the 2 slipped stitches and slip them back to left needle, P3tog, work 7 stitches in pattern; repeat from * to last 8 stitches, work another decrease as before, K3, P2. You now have 99 stitches.
SMALL COLLAR VERSION	
Next Rows	Work the 7 rows of the Collar Pattern, ending with a right-side row.
Binding off	With wrong side facing, bind off all stitches knitwise, and AT THE SAME TIME, work double decrease over the 3 stitches that form the inverted V as for side edging, keeping 5 stitches between decreases.
LARGE COLLAR VERSION	
Next Rows	Work the 7 rows of the Collar Pattern, ending with a right-side row.
NOTE	From here on you are working right-side rows on the wrong side of the poncho, so that the right side of the collar shows when the collar is turned down.
Next Row (right side)	K2, * M1, P3, K1, P3, M1, K1; repeat from * to last stitch, K1. You now have 123 stitches.
Next Row (wrong side)	Work Row 1 of Pattern 1.
Next Rows	Work 5 repeats of Pattern 1 ending with Row 5.
Binding off	Bind off knitwise in the same manner as for panel side edges.
	Weave in remaining ends. Lightly steam yoke and collar, if desired.

Glossary of Terms
Knitting and Crochet

AS ESTABLISHED. Continue working in the same manner as previous rows/rounds, whether in a stitch pattern or shaping. (*See also* Stitch Pattern.)

ASTERISK (*). (*See* Repeat.)

BIND OFF (BO). Also known as cast off. To remove knit stitches from needle in a manner that keeps them from unraveling. A common bind-off is as follows: Knit 2 stitches, insert the left-hand needle into the front loop of the stitch knit first, lift it over the stitch knit second, and remove it from the right-hand needle. Continue in this manner until you have bound off the required number of stitches. *Note:* When 1 stitch remains, cut the yarn, leaving a 6" tail, then pass the tail through the loop of the last stitch and pull to tighten. (*See also* Three-Needle Bind-Off.) ▼

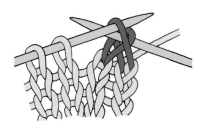

CAST ON (CO). To put stitches onto the needle to begin a knitted piece. The long-tail cast-on is one common method, and it is worked as follows: Leaving a long tail (allow approximately 1" per cast-on stitch), make a slip knot and place loop on needle. With the needle in your right hand, hold the tail and working end of the yarn in your left hand, as shown. ▼

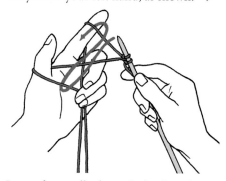

Insert the needle through the front loop of the tail on your thumb. Bring the needle tip over and behind the working yarn on your finger. Use the needle to draw the working yarn through the tail loop on your thumb. ▼

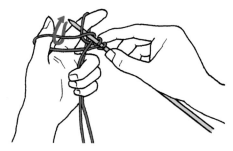

Release the tail loop on your thumb, place your thumb underneath the tail, and pull both yarns to tighten while holding both firmly against your palm. (*See also* Provisional Cast-On.) ▼

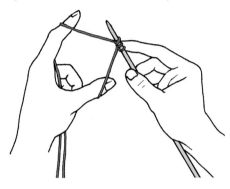

CHAIN (ch). Starting with a knotted slip stitch on the hook, yarn over and pull the yarn through the loop on the hook (1 chain made). Repeat until you have the right number of chains. ▼

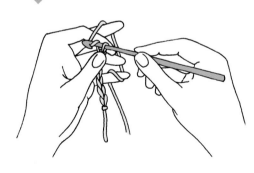

slip knot   chain on hook

To count chains, identify the front, which looks like a series of Vs. Do not count the slip knot or the chain on the hook. ▼

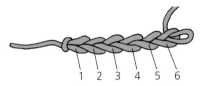
1 2 3 4 5 6

The back of the chain looks like a series of bumps. ▼

DECREASE (dec). To reduce the number of stitches being worked, 1 or 2 stitches at a time. *In knitting,* the most common way to decrease is by knitting 2 stitches together (*see* Knit 2 Stitches Together). Decreasing is different from binding off (*see* Bind Off). ▼

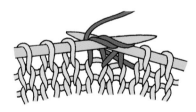

In crochet, work 2 stitches together; there are several ways to do this. In this book, most decreases are accomplished using the slip stitch (*see* Slip Stitch).

DOUBLE CROCHET (dc). After making a foundation chain, begin with a loop on the hook; yarn over, insert hook into fourth chain from the hook, yarn over, and pull up a loop (3 loops on hook); yarn over and pull through 2 of the loops on the hook (2 loops remain on hook); yarn over and pull through both loops on the hook (1 dc made). Make next dc in the next stitch of the chain. At end of row, chain 3, turn; work dc into tops of stitches from previous rows. ▼

FASTEN OFF. To end a row or round of crochet in such a way that the work will not unravel. Work until 1 loop remains on hook; cut the yarn, leaving a 6" tail. Pass the tail through loop of last stitch and pull to tighten. (*See also* Round; Row; Tail.)

FOUNDATION CHAIN. The chain worked at the beginning of a crochet piece.

GRAFTING. *In knitting,* to create a row of stitches using a threaded needle and yarn. True grafting is done on live stitches and makes a completely invisible join. These live stitches may be on the knitting needle or held on waste yarn. Grafting can be done both knitwise (shown) and purlwise.

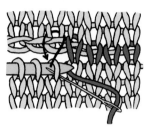

grafting stitches to stitches

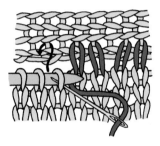

grafting stitches to rows

HALF DOUBLE CROCHET (hdc). After making a foundation chain, begin with a loop on the hook; yarn over, insert hook into third chain from the hook, yarn over, and pull up a loop (3 loops on hook); yarn over and pull hook through all 3 loops on hook (1 hdc made). Make next hdc in the next stitch of the chain. At end of row, chain 2, turn; work hdc into tops of stitches from previous row. ▼

INCREASE (inc). To add stitches, one or two at a time. *For knitting,* there are several types of increases. The two most often used in this book are Knit 1 Front and Back (K1-f/b) and Make 1 (M1, M1-L, M1-R), described in this glossary. *For crochet,* increase by working 2 or more stitches into the same stitch from the previous row, or by working into edge stitches that would otherwise be skipped. ▼

IN PATTERN. To continue working in the stitch pattern while working shaping instructions or binding off. (*See also* As Established; Bind Off.)

INTARSIA. A method of handling a color yarn that is isolated in a field of another color, distant from other repeats, or used only once. When you begin each new color, leave the old color behind and knit or crochet the next color from a new ball of yarn. Be sure to wrap the old and new yarns around each other on the wrong side of the work, as shown. This locks the yarns neatly together and

creates a strong, smooth join with no gaps in the work. ▼

JOIN NEW YARN. *In knitting,* fold the new strand 6" from the end (to leave a tail to be woven in later), place the fold on the right-hand needle, and work the next stitch. After working several stitches, pull gently on the tail of the new strand to tighten the first few stitches to the same tension as the rest of the work. *In crochet,* new yarn is commonly joined with a slip stitch, or work as follows: Work until 2 loops remain on the hook, drop the old yarn (or cut, leaving a 6" tail), and work the last 2 loops with the new yarn. (*See also* Weave in Ends.) ▼

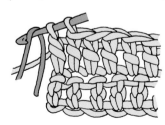

KNIT 1 FRONT AND BACK (K1-f/b).
Knit the next stitch, do not drop from left-hand needle; knit the same stitch through the back loop (tbl), drop stitch from left-hand needle. This kind of increase, also called a bar increase, leaves a small bar or bump at the base of the second stitch. ▼

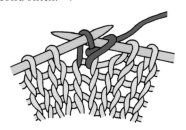

KNIT 2 STITCHES TOGETHER (K2tog).
Insert the right-hand needle into the second and first stitch on the left-hand needle at the same time. Knit them together as if they were 1 stitch. This decrease technique will make your knitting narrower by removing stitches. ▼

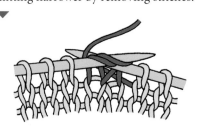

KNIT 3 STITCHES TOGETHER (K3tog).
For this decrease, insert the right needle into 3 stitches at once and knit them together. This makes a thick asymmetrical decrease that slants to the right. ▼

MAKE 1 (M1, M1-L, M1-R).
Insert the tip of the left-hand needle front to back into the strand of yarn between the stitch just worked and the next stitch. Lift strand, place it on left-hand needle, then knit it through the back loop, twisting it to close the hole. The resulting stitch slants to the left and is called M1-L. ▼

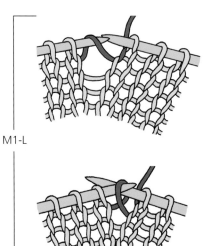

M1-L

For a right-slanting stitch (M1-R), pick up the strand from back to front and knit it through the front loop, twisting the strand to prevent a hole. (*See also* Increase; Through the Back Loop.) ▼

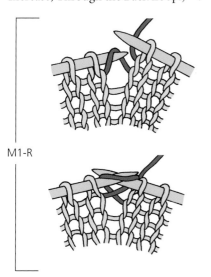

M1-R

MARKER. Used to indicate pattern sections or to mark the beginning of a round when working circularly. *In knitting,* use either ring markers or split-ring markers. *In crochet,* use only split-ring markers, as they have to be moved from the marked stitch row by row. (*See also* Round.) ▼

knitting marker

crochet markers

MULTIPLE. The number of stitches required to complete a single set of knit or crochet pattern stitches.

PASS THE SLIPPED STITCH OVER (psso). Used in knitting when decreasing. Slip 1 stitch, knit the next stitch, then use the left-hand needle to lift the slipped stitch over the knit stitch and drop it off the needle. (*See also* Slip, slip, knit.) ▼

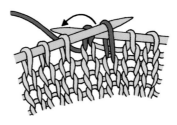

PICK UP STITCHES. To begin a new section of the piece by picking up along a knit (or crocheted) edge, using a knitting needle or a crochet hook, as follows: *Needle method:* Hold the needle in your right hand and work from right to left. With the right side facing you, insert the needle into the first stitch, wrap the yarn around the needle, and draw the yarn through as for a normal knit stitch. Continue until you have the required number of stitches. You may also used this method to pick up stitches from the back of a crocheted chain (known as one of the provisional cast-ons). *Tip:* If it's difficult to work with only one needle, hold a second needle in your left hand and use it to pick up the stitch so that you can knit it with the right-hand needle. ▼

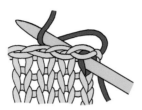

Hook method: Hold the knitting needle in your left hand and work from left to right. Insert the hook into the first stitch, wrap yarn around the hook, and pull through a loop (first stitch). Place this stitch onto the needle. Repeat until you have the required number of stitches.

▼

PICOT. A small loop or other decorative pattern stitch, usually used on edges of pieces. (See photo on page 24.)

PLACE ON HOLDER. To remove a stitch or section of stitches that will not be worked for several rows or that will be used later during finishing and hold them on either a stitch holder or a piece of waste yarn until needed.

PROVISIONAL CAST-ON. *In knitting,* used to provide an edge for live stitches to be worked later. One method is to first crochet a chain (*see* Chain). Using waste yarn and an appropriately sized hook, chain the number of stitches specified. (*Tip:* It's good insurance to work a few extra chains; these are easy to remove later.) With a knitting needle and working yarn, pick up and knit the required number of stitches from the back of the crocheted chain. ▼

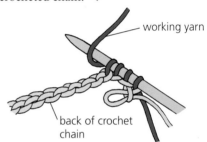

working yarn

back of crochet chain

When ready to work into these stitches, unravel the chain and place the live stitches on the needle. ▼

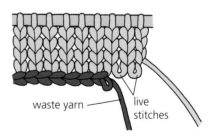

waste yarn

live stitches

PURL 2 STITCHES TOGETHER (P2tog). Insert the right-hand needle into both of the next 2 stitches on the left-hand needle as if to purl, then purl them together as if they were 1 stitch. (*See also* Decrease.) ▼

REPEAT. To work the indicated number of stitches (usually the stitch pattern multiple), either after an asterisk * or enclosed in brackets [ ] or parentheses ( ), the number of times specified in the instructions. *Note:* Some patterns state the *total* number of times to work the instructions; others state the number of times to repeat the instructions *after* working the repeat the first time. A † within a stitch pattern repeat indicates that the last time the stitch pattern repeat is worked, it should be worked only to that point, and then the row/round should be completed by working the instructions that follow.

REVERSE STOCKINETTE STITCH. When working straight, purl all stitches on right-side rows, knit all stitches on wrong-side rows; when working in the round, purl all stitches every round. (*See* Stockinette Stitch.)

RIGHT SIDE. The side of the fabric meant to be the "public" side. In a garment, it is the side worn facing out, away from the body.

RING. *In crochet,* to begin a ring, chain 4, then insert your hook into the first chain. Yarn over, then draw the yarn through both the chain and the loop on the hook with no further yarn overs. ▼

ROUND. A round begins and ends at the same point. *In knitting,* a round is complete when all stitches have been worked once when working circularly (with a circular needle or double-pointed needles). It's helpful to use a marker to indicate the beginning and end of the rounds. ▼

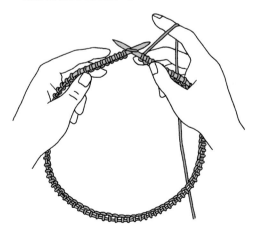

In crochet, a round is complete when all stitches have been worked without turning. You may indicate the end of the round with a marker and join the round with a slip stitch or you may work rounds in a continuous spiral. (*See also* Marker.) ▼

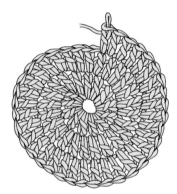

continuous spiral

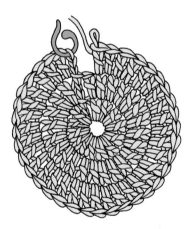

completing a circular round

ROW. One row is complete when you have worked straight from the first stitch to the last stitch.

SINGLE CROCHET (sc). After making a foundation chain, begin with a loop on the hook; insert hook into second chain from the hook, yarn over, and pull up a loop (2 loops on hook); yarn over and pull yarn through both loops on hook (1 sc made). Make next sc in next stitch of the chain. At the end of row, chain 1, turn; work sc into tops of stitches from previous row. ▼

SLIP MARKER. *In knitting,* move the marker from the left-hand needle to the right-hand needle and continue working. *In crochet,* move the marker from the marked stitch up to the next row/ round. (*See also* Marker.)

SLIP, SLIP, KNIT (ssk). Slip 2 stitches, one at a time as if to knit, to the right-hand needle. Return them to the left-hand needle in turned position, then knit them together through the back loops. *Tip:* To avoid stretching the leading stitch, work with just the tip of the needles. ▼

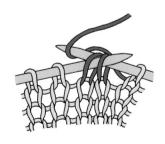

SLIP STITCH. *In knitting,* moving a stitch from the left-hand needle to the right without working it. This can be done knitwise or purlwise. ▼

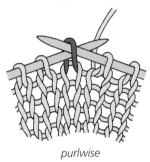

purlwise

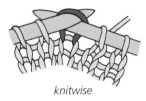

knitwise

In crochet, a way of either joining or moving across a stitch without adding height. Insert hook into top of stitch and draw yarn through both top loop of stitch and loop on hook without any yarn overs. ▼

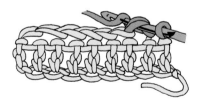

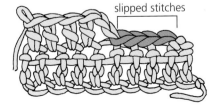

slipped stitches

SPACE. *In crochet,* the eyelet (hole) created when a series of chains were worked in the preceding row or round. Instructions may indicate that you crochet into a space rather than into a stitch.

STITCH PATTERN. A number of stitches worked over one or more rows or rounds in a specific sequence, to produce the texture of the fabric unique to the piece being knitted or crocheted. The instructions indicate how many stitches are in the stitch pattern and how many times to repeat the sequence. (*See also* Multiple; Repeat.)

STOCKINETTE STITCH. *In knitting,* when working straight, knit all stitches on right-side rows and purl all stitches on wrong-side rows. When working in the round, knit all stitches every round. ▼

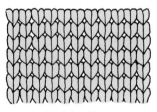

right side

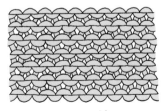

wrong side

TAIL. A strand of yarn, 6" or more in length, left when beginning and ending use of that yarn. *In knitting,* this occurs when casting on and binding off. *In crochet,* tails remain from the foundation chain and when fastening off. *In both knitting and crochet,* you also have tails when you join a new ball of yarn or change colors within a row or round. You can either neatly weave in the tail during finishing or use it to sew seams or reinforce color joins. (*See also* Weave in Ends.)

THREE-NEEDLE BIND-OFF. Also known as a knitted seam. Used in knitting to bind off and join two pieces together at the same time. To work: Place the stitches of the pieces to be joined on separate needles (or on each end of a circular needle). Hold both needles in left hand, one behind the other, with the right sides of the pieces facing each other. With a third needle in your right hand (the same size or one size larger than the needles you used to knit the piece), knit 2 stitches together, one from the front needle and one from the back needle, onto the right-hand needle. Repeat with the next stitches on each needle, then pass the first stitch over the second and off the right-hand needle: 1 stitch bound off. Continue until you have 1 stitch left. Cut yarn, leaving a tail

for weaving in; pull tail through last loop and fasten off. (*See also* Bind Off; Knit 2 Stitches Together; Right Side.) ▼

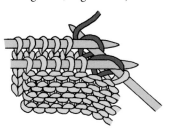

THROUGH THE BACK LOOP (tbl). Insert the right-hand needle into the part of the next stitch that lies behind the left-hand needle and work from that position. Working stitches through the back loops results in twisted stitches, a decorative feature of some stitch patterns. ▼

knit 1 tbl

purl 2 together tbl

TRIPLE CROCHET (tr). After making a foundation chain, begin with a loop on the hook; yarn over twice, insert hook into fifth chain from the hook, yarn over, and pull up a loop (4 loops on hook); yarn over and pull through 2 loops on hook (3 loops now on hook); yarn over and pull through 2 loops on hook (2 loops now on hook); yarn over once more and pull yarn through last 2 loops on the hook. Make next tr in next stitch of the chain. At end of row, chain 4, turn; work tr into tops of stitches from previous row. ▼

TURN. Work across all stitches to the end of the row, or to the point specified in the instructions, then rotate the piece so that the opposite side of the work is facing. When working straight, turn at the end of every row in both knitting and crochet, unless the instructions state otherwise. (*See also* Row.)

TURNING CHAIN. *In crochet*, one or more chains worked at the beginning of a row or round to raise the next row or round up to the appropriate level for working. The pattern stitch determines the number of chains required for the turning chain. The turning chain that begins the next row is sometimes counted as the first stitch(es) of the next row/round. This will be stated in parentheses in the directions the first time it occurs, but may not be stated on subsequent rows or rounds. (*See also* Chain; Stitch Pattern.) ▼

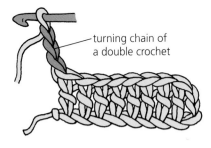

turning chain of a double crochet

WASTE YARN. Use waste yarn (small bits of yarn left over from previous projects) as stitch markers or stitch holders as well as for working a provisional cast-on in knitting. (*See also* Provisional Cast-On.)

WEAVE IN ENDS. This is done to secure tails left when beginning and ending a piece or when joining new yarn. *In knitting*, the tail can be woven along the same row of stitches, using a large-eye needle. ▼

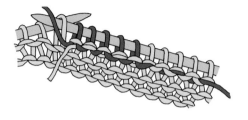

In crochet, thread the tail on a yarn needle; neatly run the end in and out of a few stitches on the wrong side of the piece. (*See also* Join New Yarn; Tail.) ▼

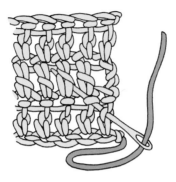

WRONG SIDE. The side of the fabric meant to be the "private" side. In a garment, the wrong side is worn against the body; in a stitch pattern, the less attractive side may be designated as the wrong side.

YARN OVER (yo). *In knitting,* bring the yarn to the front between the needles (to the purl position, if it is not already there); lift it up and over the needle to the knit position, then place it in the correct position to work the next stitch. ▼

In crochet, wrap the yarn around the hook so that the strand is caught in the head of the hook, then draw the yarn through as specified in the instructions. (May also be stated as *yarn over hook* or *yarn around hook.*) ▼

To Meg, my muse.

Acknowledgments

So many thanks to Nancy and Gwen, who maintained grace under pressure,
and to all the designers who worked so fast, then waited patiently.
The test knitters and crocheters were spectacular. Thanks to Emily Burkholder,
Kaedean Doppelmayr, Meg Eckman, Etta Hallock, Janet Kallstrom, Grace Miser,
Elaine Slyper, and Diana Foster for their nimble fingers and eagle eyes.

Resources

Artyarns, Inc.
39 Westmoreland Avenue
White Plains, NY 10606
(914) 428-0333
www.artyarns.com
(Project: Starlet Shrug)

Berroco, Inc.
14 Elmdale Road
P.O. Box 367
Uxbridge, MA 01569-0367
www.berroco.com
(Projects: Mossy Stole, Faux Fur Muffler,
Golden Mesh Wrap)

Brown Sheep Company, Inc.
100662 CR 16
Mitchell, NE 69357-2136
(308) 635-2143
www.brownsheep.com
(Project: Snug Fall Cozy)

Classic Elite Yarns
300 Jackson Street
Lowell, MA 01852-2108
(978) 453-2837
www.classiceliteyarns.com
(Projects: Shirred Scarf, Maid Marian
Cloak)

Country Needleworks
584 Chicago Drive
Jenison, MI 49428
www.countryneedleworks.net
616-457-9410

Dale of Norway
N16 W23390 Stoneridge Drive #A
Waukesha, WI 53188-1108
(262) 544-1996
www.daleofnorway.com
(Project: Aran Poncho)

JCA, Inc.
35 Scales Lane
Townsend, MA 01469-1011
(800) 225-6340
www.jcacrafts.com
(Project: Meg's Poncho)

JHB International, Inc.
1955 S. Quince Street
Denver, CO 80231-3206
(303) 751-8100
www.buttons.com
(Project: Meg's Poncho)

K1C2
2220 Eastman Avenue #106
Ventura, CA 93003
(Project: Shirred Scarf)

Kaleidoscope Yarns
15 Pearl Street
Essex Junction, VT 05452
www.kyarns.com
(802) 288-9200

Knitting Fever/Euro Yarns
35 Debevoise Avenue
Roosevelt, NY 11575-1711
(516) 546-3600
www.knittingfever.com
(Projects: Rainbow Poncho and
Rainbow Leggings)

Lorna's Laces
4229 N. Honore Street
Chicago, IL 60613-1074
(773) 935-3803
www.lornaslaces.net
(Project: Cinderella Cape)

Not Just Yarn
20 Technology Drive
Brattleboro, VT 05301
www.notjustyarn.com
(802) 257-1145

Plymouth Yarn Company
P.O. Box 28
Bristol, PA 19007
(Projects: Coral Capelet, Rainbow
Gauntlets)

Quietly Wild Yarn & Craft Store
114 South Jefferson Street
Woodstock, IL 60098
(815) 337-2400
www.wildyarn.com

Spirit Trail Fiberworks
P.O. Box 197
Sperryville, VA 22740
www.spirit-trail.net
(703) 309-3199

Trendsetter Yarns
16745 Saticoy Street #101
Van Nuys, CA 91406-2710
(818) 780-5497
www.trendsetteryarns.com
(Project: Electric Cowgirl)

Unicorn Books & Crafts, Inc.
1338 Ross Street
Petaluma, CA 94954-1117
(707) 762-3362
www.unicornbooks.com
(Project: Upcountry Poncho)

Webs
75 Service Center Road
Northampton, MA 01061
www.yarn.com
(800) 367-9327

Yarns Etc.
231 South Elm Street
Greensboro, NC 27401
www.yarnsetc.com
(336) 370-1233

Index